"A man has maybe seventy years of
living to do. He can live it
with joy or he can be a sad little
soul with bile in his guts and
fear for a friend. No matter
which way he goes, it's his life
and nobody else can live it for him."

> Peter Thayne Conroy
> (the grandfather)

"The bloody human race is a dim
experiment that failed several
hundred years ago."

> Hal Conroy
> (the grandson)

"Mine enemy grows older."

> Alexander King

A MUG OF BOATY TEA

Hal Conroy

PaperJacks

A division of General Publishing Co. Limited

Published 1972 in PaperJacks,
A division of General Publishing Co. Limited,
30 Lesmill Road, Don Mills, Ontario

Text illustrations by Lionel Alldred

Cover and title page illustrations
by the author

ISBN 0-7737-7022-4

Printed in Canada

This book is for

Lionel and Pam

two beloved friends

who have given of themselves

and

Jim Glass, Sea Scout Master

writer and damn good friend

PROLOGUE

A number of years ago, just after the war
as a matter of fact, a great many people
sailed small boats across the Atlantic from
England. Most of them were ex-service officers, mostly Navy and several -- myself
included - Merchant Navy officers.

There were so many of us that the story
is told of a single-handed ocean sailor
who was trying to impress a young woman.
He eyed the cleavage of her dress with a
practised eye and purred "M'dear, I've just
sailed me boat singlehanded from Portsmouth
to New York."

To which the young woman replied in bored
tones, "Doesn't everybody."

Now, I'm not trying to impress any young
lady with cleavage when I mutter with a
little modest pride, "M'dear, I've just
been writing me a book," but it wouldn't
surprise me one damn bit if she replied,
"Doesn't everybody."

But the fact that everybody seems to
write books notwithstanding, at least I may
lay claim to the fact that I am a professional writer - although this is my first
book.

It is a small book because I believe that
once you have said what you have to say you
should put the cover back on the typewriter
and not clatter on.

It is a meandering sort of book, but then,
the small voyage was a meander. I make
some rather snarky observations about people
and cities and about many other things, but
that is because it is the way I feel.

I don't think I have been overly profound, kindly-minded, or Great Writerish, but I have had things to say and I have said them.

I make no apology for what I have written in this book. Some of what I have had to say I suppose may sound bigoted, reactionary, terribly Right, and downright arrogant. This may be true, but this book is about me and the things I have done and the people I have done them with. A man cannot change his personality to suit his writing, and what he writes, if he is an honest writer, is what he is.

While the book is true, I have changed names, dates, and sometimes places for some good reasons.

I shall send a copy of this book to a certain gentleman of the Canada Council who rejected this on the grounds – I'd applied for a small grant – that it was a "Manual for Navigation" and then added insult to idiocy by saying that, inasmuch as I'd been a newspaperman for some twenty years, I wasn't a Creative Writer.

Whatever the hell that is ... a Creative Writer?

The same booby – or one like him – not many months later gave a grant of Five Thousand Dollars to a clown from the West Coast – where most Canadian-type clowns are from – for a short story about the size of the sexual organs of Billy the Kid.

As a non-Creative Writer I wouldn't have minded so much if that writer had picked Louis Riel – at least HE was a Canadian; but this whatever-the-hell-he-is got five grand for a story about a third-rate hood from Brooklyn, New York.

As my grandfather would have said, "Bad cess to him, the bloody little blatherskite."

Hal Conroy
Montreal, 1972

CHAPTER ONE

It is, I suppose, rather strange that a man
who was born and brought up in the prairie
country should have been a Merchant Navy
officer from his thirteenth year to his
twenty-seventh, but during World War Two
most of the officers and men of the
R.C.N.V.R. came from the prairie provinces.
Don't ask me to explain it, but there it
is. Oh yes, before I forget, Manitoba
does have a seaport.

Anyway, as a child I wasn't too interested in the sea or in boats, although I
loved to sit on the forbidden-by-my-mother
banks of the Red River and dream.

Both Father and Grandfather were soldiers, and because I spent a great deal of
my childhood around army barracks - like
Fort Osborne in Winnipeg - I lived, dreamed and played soldier.

My only toys were soldiers or things that
I could relate to army life - my trains
were all turned into troop-trains, armour-
ed trains, or mobile artillery.

My presents - and there were a lot of
them on my birthday or at Christmas -
either Father and his friends or Grandfather and his would give me toy soldiers,
artillery, lorries, tanks ... all in scale.
I would pack them in a special box that
Grandfather had made for me and I would
load them in the trailer - an old child's
go-cart that Grandfather had converted for
fitting to the rear of my bike - take a
lunch, a couple of books, and away I'd go
to my very favourite secret place.

"Those of us who mess about in boats
are truly touched with madness."

It was the remains of an old stone farm-house out at a place that no longer exists. Crow's Bush was located at the northwest end of West Kildonan. Its southern border was a disused railroad track that ran east to Transcona and west to I-never-found-out. The east border was the CPR tracks, which ran north to Winnipeg Beach, a popular resort for middle-class Winnipeggers in the thirties ... unlike Grand Beach on the east side of Lake Winnipeg, Winnipeg Beach allowed Jews to rent property. Mother hated the place because of this, and some of that hate rubbed off on me. I often used one of my mother's favourite remarks: "I wouldn't wipe my shoes on them ... her ... him ... those people . . the Jews ... the Bohunks ..."

Also I remember a sign at the head of the street we lived on during some of our summers in Grand Beach. It read: "GENTILES ONLY".

And as I recall, most of Grand Beach was owned by the Canadian National Railways.

We lived, I think, in an age of innocent intolerance. By innocent intolerance, I mean that my father as well as hundreds and hundreds of other men referred to all rail-way porters as "George". They meant nothing by it and where the habit came from I don't know. And while it possibly was patronizing, I feel it was much better than saying, "Here, boy," as I heard innumerable times when I was in India during the war.

West Kildonan, where I lived when I was a boy, was a tight little Anglo-Saxon cul-de-sac in the north end of Winnipeg, and before we could get to the rest of Winni-peg we had to pass through a very large Jewish district, a German district, and a Ukrainian district. I think the Jews occupied the area that ran from Selkirk Avenue north to about College Street and west to Saeter Street. The Germans and

11

Ukrainians had an uneasy alliance farther
west and north of that, and I might add
that the Ukrainian market gardeners and
farmers sort of surrounded us Anglo-Saxons
in West Kildonan.

I don't think I remember ever seeing a
Negro in West Kildonan. As a matter of
fact, there were no Negroes in West Kildonan, and once when a Sunday school picnic
from a Negro Baptist church - which had
been built by the railway porters of the
American and Canadian railroads near the
CPR station - was held in Kildonan Park, a
number of us, aged ten, eleven, and twelve,
watched in awe, because here were all these
coloured kids doing the same things at
their Sunday school picnic that we had been
doing at our United Church Sunday school
picnic, and when I remarked on this phen-
omenon to my grandfather, he looked at me
for a moment and said, "What the devil do
you think they do, swing from the bloody
trees?"

And speaking of our United Church Sunday
school, I have noticed within the last
couple of years a number of Jewish organizations here in Canada accuse the United
Church's official publication, "The Obser-
ver", and some of the Church's ministers
of being anti-Semitic, and while I can't
say whether or not this is true, I do
recall a Sunday school concert where a
group of us got up on the stage and pran-
ced about singing a song, "Ikey, Smikey,
dirty old Ikey", and one of my Sunday
school teachers of the period, who shall
be nameless though the lady has long since
gone to her possibly just reward, told us
quite earnestly that the Jews were very
naughty because they had killed Christ.
We impressionable ten- and eleven-year-
olds thought this over the next day. About
six of us, reinforced by some of our other
friends, including one who might be called

12

West Kildonan's token Jew, spotted an old Jewish junk man coming down the back lane behind my house. We immediately attacked him, throwing stones and screaming, "You killed Christ, you killed Christ!" Suddenly all of us were simultaneously struck by the same blow. My grandfather had come upon us. Those of us who did not escape spent the rest of the morning wandering up and down the sun-drenched (it was July) back lanes of West Kildonan pawing through the garbage while my grandfather and the elderly Jewish gentleman sat in the wagon sharing a bottle of Manechewitz wine, and occasionally my grandfather would pick up the long whip and flick it none too gently over our sweating adolescent backsides.

I might add that none of the kids dared tell their parents what happened, but Grandfather informed my mother about my foray into the garbage cans of West Kildonan. She went into deep shock and didn't speak to anybody in our house for three days.

But to return to the toy soldiers who were almost the only playmates I ever had. Once out to the farm, I would repair any damage to the trenches - about two inches deep, with firing steps, dugouts, and everything - that I had dug in the soft clay. In would go the troops. British in one line and the tiny German soldiers in the other. The no-man's land between the trenches was pitted with shell holes, smashed guns, and barbed wire I'd made by tying knots in silver thread and fitting it to match sticks. There were even a few "bodies" of dead soldiers lying in or out of the shell holes. I'd lined the holes with bits of heavy canvas so that the holes would hold water just like the ones in the pictures in my war books. I had learned that if you broke the head off the little soldiers you could insert a wooden match

13

stick into the body and the head, and thus you'd have a few troops who could turn their heads.

Both sides had general staffs on horseback, with calvary escorts. These, like their Great War – as we then called World War One – counterparts, were well behind the lines. The tiny field guns could fire small "ladyfinger" firecrackers and I became rather adept at rapid-firing my two sets of guns. Sometimes the "shells" would burst in mid air or they'd land in a trench, burst, and cause casualties. The trenches would be repaired and the dead buried ... somewhere in the middle of what is now a bloody street full of middle-class houses are the graves of my brave dead from both sides ... I really buried the ones who had powder burns on their bodies. A soldier who was knocked over was merely wounded. The horse-drawn ambulance would cart him off to the hospital tent – real tent, real canvas – that was staffed by inch-high doctors.

From the time I was in my tenth summer until my thirteenth, I spent many days at war. Nobody ever came near the place, I don't think anyone knew it existed. I would leave a few troops in both sets of trenches and when I'd return they'd always be there, some standing on the fire steps, the sitting ones crouched in the dugouts, an officer peering at the enemy through his field glasses, and there might be a little more water in the shell holes.

I know what the head doctors would say about me. The "Trick Cyclists", as the British sailors so aptly call them, would maintain that I played war because in my subconscious I was killing all the people I didn't like ... balderdash, fellows, and dark green snuff to your dumb old hypothesis. I did that when I sat daydreaming at the site for the new sewage disposal

plant ... there just HAS to be some sort
of psychological connection there. When I
played war, I was the General who directed
battles, a great gaunt figure on a grey
horse ... I liked to think that I looked
and acted like Kitchener, a man who had no
time for petty people, a bemedaled, red-
tabbed super-general who advised kings.

I was too busy winning a war to be concerned with the warped souls who tormented
a small boy.

To be honest about it, other children had
tried to befriend me, but I wanted none of
it. I was afraid of them, for until my
father had returned to the army I'd spent
my summers living in the "Super's" private
railway home-on-tracks, for my father was
employed as a super-foreman on one of the
lines that the CPR was running across Manitoba, Saskatchewan, and Alberta during
the time when the world was sane and certain kinds of people knew their proper
place in the Order of Life. In the winter,
we lived in the Coronet Hotel in Winnipeg
... I didn't know what other children
looked like.

This life lasted from the time I was
three until I was seven, then Father went
back into the army with the rank of Captain ... when the 1914-18 war had ended,
he'd been a Major. Other children scared
the hell out of me and school was a tor-
ment.

I took the easy way out, I refused to
play with ANYBODY. My parents would give
me birthday parties and after the party
got going I'd go to the cellar or the attic
and do what I wanted to do, be alone and
read a book or play with my puppet theatre
... puppets didn't call you Cissy Conroy
and hit you. Lead soldiers didn't take
your candy away from you and tease you.
When you sat on a river bank, the water
didn't give you a bloody nose and laugh at
you.

15

I felt lonely but it was safer to be lonely than it was to have to fight the whole damn world. So, I retreated into a beautiful world of brave deeds, of cliff-climbing, of sitting and watching the river flow by, and of not taking chances with other children, for children are the most cruel, ugly little beings on God's green earth. Even I was cruel.

I had a complete regiment of troops in tropic gear. They wore shorts and pith helmets and they had camels. There was a creek running through the old farm and its banks were sandy. The creek became the White Nile and the troops were on their way to avenge General Gordon. There were a great many grasshoppers that summer, and, because they looked sort of human if you stood them on end, they became the Dervish members of Mahdi's army. I would capture them, tie them to a stake, put paper around them, and if they refused to divulge the whereabouts of the Mahdi and his Emirs I'd order them burned at the stake. There is no record of the British doing this to its fuzzy-wuzzy enemies but there is the record of tying Indian - Hindu - rebels to gun barrels and firing eighteen-pound shells through them. I improvised by tying a grasshopper to the mouth of one of my tiny artillery pieces and then inserting a fire-cracker into the gun, lighting it, and blowing a bit of a hole in the poor grass-hopper.

This nasty little game came to an end when I burned my own hand and got some idea of what the poor bloody grasshopper must have suffered at my ten-year-old hands.

There is this streak in each of us. It is bad enough in a small boy, but I know of a place where some young adult males used live chickens to break windows. This doesn't excuse me but I was ten and these were insects - in their case, the boys

16

were over twenty ...

However, this is the only time in my childhood that I was cruel to a living creature. I remember that I once found a dying bird and I cried while I asked God to cure it. Later I gave it a military funeral complete with a band and put it under a small Union Jack on a gun carriage. Even the murdered Cock-Robin didn't get a send-off like that.

I did have some friends, of course - one, Danny Dack, was the son of West Kildonan's leading druggist ... My other friend was Oscar Dagner; he grew up to become the building superintendent at the Winnipeg Post Office. Both boys, like myself, were loners.

But my best friend and the one person I really trusted was my grandfather, Peter Thayne Conroy, soldier, adventurer, lover, scholar - and most of all, Man.

I loved him, respected him, sometimes I feared his wrath, but most of all I trusted him. He was big, about six-two, with piercing brown eyes, dark brown hair cut close to the head. He always wore army shirts and corduroy pants when he was out of uniform. He never went out of doors without wearing a tie or, if the shirt collar was open, a scarf made of fine white silk. His boots were always polished to a high gloss and his canes - he had a large collection of them - were always kept polished. He wore tweeds when he wanted to dress up and his hats were either battered looking tweeds or a tam-'o-shanter with a small British flag sown where a badge is usually worn.

His mode of dress left a lasting impression on me because I now, as I have for many years, dress the same way...

He had a soft Irish brogue and a none-too-soft Irish temper. He loved a good fight, either with words or with fists. He was

17

rugged, stubborn, kind, mean-tempered, and he stood head and shoulders above all other men. He loved women and he made love to them, but he also respected them. Once he said to me, "Me boy, it does not matter if a woman be a saint or what some men call sluts, they are women and as such should be treated with kindness and respect." His feelings always were that if a woman were good enough to go to bed with a man she should be good enough to be seen walking down the street with him.

He never just got mad ... he got mad with a plan. A gentle man, he could turn into a brutal savage at the drop of a word. I remember seeing him beat a drunk to a bloody pulp once, just because that drunk had cursed an Indian prostitute. Grandfather gave the onlookers the impression that he was in a towering, screaming, murderous rage. Murderous he was, but in a rage - no. The roarings, the shakings with rage were for the benefit of the people watching the fight. In point of fact, Grandfather was as cool as an arctic summer. Every move he made was planned so that what looked like blind rage was a carefully drawn up strategy.

When the fight was over - it lasted about four minutes - the drunk was injured so badly that he had to be taken to the hospital, and, because half the Winnipeg police force were Irish and the other half had been in the army with Grandfather, the police report read that the drunk had "fallen down a flight of stairs while impaired." If he was a smart drunk, he accepted the police report.

I might add that over the years a great many drunks fell down stairs in Winnipeg. Grandfather hated drunks. I take after him.

"A drunk, my boy, is a foul blot on the human race and a disgrace to the God who created him. He should be beaten and kicked by every decent citizen who encounters him when he is in that rotten condition."

To Grandfather, the A.A. and the Salvation Army with its "Harbour Lights" missions were wrong and should be stopped. God help the drunk that dared to stop and ask him for a dime. Grandfather would smile, pretend to be reaching for the dime, and then - WHAM - the poor devil would land on his back on the sidewalk and would be damn lucky if he didn't get a busted jaw.

Grandfather was a law unto himself.

And yet, there was many a drunk's family who ate, had their rent paid or clothes put on their backs by the very man who had smashed up the drunken husband and father. Grandfather was an intolerant man ... he was not, in his lights, always right ... but he was never wrong. He'd break a man, then lend him a dollar to get home.

And he hated the Americans, which he didn't bother to hide from an American daughter-in-law.

But he did understand a lonely little boy whose real world was one in which toy soldiers had souls and whose pretend world was one where humankind was cruel to small boys. He watched a mother who would insist that a five-year-old learn to read and then force the teachers to put him in grade two instead of grade one. He watched and waited until the boy was ten and the mother bored with playing Mama and then he made his move.

With Irish skill and clever words he flattered the woman he hated. He pointed out that she was too young to have to bother with bringing up a small boy, that we should have a maid ... we got one, a long-limbed beauty from the steppes of Russia with a beautiful bust and a flashing smile for the great Irish charmer who

19

paid her wages and who made love to her
every weekend while my mother played Great
Lady and my father sipped one beer in the
officers' mess.

Then he took me on camping trips, on long
hikes. We'd follow the hydro power lines,
those great steel towers that seemed to
stretch endlessly across the flat lands
north then west and east across the land.
He taught me how to watch an ant hill, to
spend hours watching gophers at play. He
taught me to love the great white gulls
that lived along the Red River.

Then we found the boat.

We had gone hiking along the path that
lined the west bank of the Red River. North
we went, away from the golf course, past
the bridge that connected the unused rail-
way to Transcona and then, all of a sudden,
there it was. To my ten-year-old eyes, it
was huge. It was an old Red River steam-
er, a paddle-wheeler with a great long
stack and a wheelhouse that would have
pleased that old river pilot, Sam Clemens.

God only knows how long she'd been sitting there, but there she lay, perched
alongside the bank in the mud. Her once-
gleaming white sides were grey with age,
some of the windows in the wheelhouse and
the passengers' saloons were broken but
her great stern paddle was intact, and the
quartermaster's pride and joy, the great
ship's wheel, much taller than one skinny
ten-year-old, was in place.

There were cabins with bunks and chairs
in them. There was a great - to my eyes -
dining saloon with a horseshoe of table,
no chairs. The captain's cabin with its
rich teakwood still shining was untouched,
AND - there was one lifeboat still hang-
ing in the davits.

It was the Easter holiday and I was free
from hated school, and Grandfather, who
had invested well and had escaped the '29

crash, was in this warm spring of 1930 forty-seven years of age. He had married at the tender age of fifteen because he had loved too well and his father and the father of the bride had agreed that marriage was the only answer. Four months after the blushing and somewhat pregnant bride had stood in front of a wandering Methodist circuit rider, my father was born. The year was 1899.

Despite the somewhat unromantic beginning, Grandfather loved Grandmother very deeply, and when she was killed in the Halifax explosion Grandfather mourned her for two years.

Father was afraid of him and he jumped when Grandfather roared. Father was a little afraid of me too, I think, because he never seemed to want to get really close to me. He loved me in his fashion, but like most men of his time he didn't understand children. To Mother, I was something that had happened one night and messed up her social life for nine months.

Grandfather didn't need to work for a living so he had plenty of time to devote to me. As I ran from stem to stern on the old river boat a plan was being born in my grandfather's mind. The boat would become a secret place for him and me to come to ... also it would be a great spot to bring his young woman. He called to me and once on shore we made our way towards the road that ran north to Middle Church, Selkirk, and Winnipeg Beach. We were looking for the owner of the land on whose bank the boat was sitting.

It didn't take us long to find the owner and it didn't take Grandfather too long to make a deal with the man who owned the ramshackle farm. In point of fact, I have the feeling that the whole deal was a little dishonest. The man owned the land

... later Grandfather took over the mort-
gage ... and in the end — the land. Why
the boat was there was never brought to
light.

Anyway, Grandfather set to work and fixed
up the old beauty. No longer did we hike
the six miles from West Kildonan, we drove
in Grandfather's great black Essex. He
hired a watchman, an old army buddy who
lived aboard with his wife and who stayed
out of our way. Grandfather had the grand
manner about him, he was kind but never
consorted with underlings and hirelings.

We lowered the lifeboat and discovered
that it was free of dryrot. Grandfather
and I set to work to build us a cruising
sailboat. I didn't know it then but I was
to become part of a group of men who live
all over the world ... the men who convert
lifeboats.

On that bright spring morning my grandfather took me back to our boat and made
me promise to keep my usually flapping
mouth shut because my mother, who was
afraid of water, would foul up the whole
deal.

Mother never did learn about the "Mark
Twain", as Grandfather christened the old
paddle-wheeler. The best part of all was
the "Argosy", the converted lifeboat that
Grandfather and I spent every night and
weekend working on. Grandfather was one
thing I never have been — good with his
hands. I helped, of course, but Grandfather knew a lack of talent when he saw
it so he kept me busy at the little jobs.

By the second week of May, the cabin was
finished, the hull painted black with gold
trim, and she was ready to have a shakedown
cruise. School had become a living hell
for me so Grandfather, pulling strings and
knowing where a lot of bodies were buried,
was able to arrange for me to have a private tutor and be taken out of school. The

tutor was a gentle English type who had
been an Oxford don. He was unable to cope
- as a teacher - with Canadian school children. Grandfather fixed it that he would
live aboard the "Twain" and spend his days
at our house teaching me the love of English and English authors. Mother approved
this move of my grandfather's because she
felt it gave her standing in West Kildonan.
After all, I was the only child with a real
English tutor in the whole of Winnipeg.

I will admit that I got a lot of pleasure from seeing my former schoolmates
trudging their weary and unwilling way to
school while I prepared for a day of teach-
ing-in-the-sun.

Such as I are the cause of People's Up-
risings being born.

Father merely obeyed my grandfather's
orders.

It was a beautiful morning and Grandfather, Robert, and I prepared to set sail
for Selkirk, then the heart of the Lake
Winnipeg fishing industry. For the first
time I was able to see what the cabin of
a small boat was really like. Neat little
bookshelves lined the port bulkhead. Two
gimballed lamps hung over the bunks. My
bunk was forward in the forepeak and I
also had a gimballed lamp. A table that
hung by ropes was drawn up to the deckhead and a small coal-and-wood-burning
ship's stove imported from Nova Scotia was
snugly tucked away next to the tiny head
... Grandfather cursed that thing for
years. Under the bunks with their thick
kapok-filled mattresses were lockers, and
there was a sink made from an enamel wash-
basin with a hole drilled in it. A large
cork served as a plug.

There was a suit of sails made from the
finest Irish linen - seven pieces from my
mother's unused collection of linen had
been borrowed by Grandfather and me on a

bright and early Sunday morning. Grandfather had found a sailmaker at the Winnipeg Canoe Club who'd turned that old lifeboat into a black beauty with a standing
lug. At four-thirty of the sixteenth day
of May, 1930, Grandfather cracked a bottle
of rum on "Argosy's" bow and slid her into
the water. I was a thrilled and happy
little boy.

Late that night we tied up along the
east bank of the Red. The lamps were lit,
and Grandfather and Robert smoked their
pipes ... to allow me to feel grown up,
Grandfather allowed me to suck on a cheap
(25¢) pipe that he'd bought for me when he
caught me with one of his precious Dun-
hills stuck in my mouth. We held great
enamel mugs of real boaty tea in our hands,
and a plate of thick meat sandwiches lay
on the gently swinging table. It was snug
and warm in that cabin and a happy child
fell asleep with a half-eaten sandwich
clutched in his hand.

When I look back on those summers that
lasted until 1934, I am sure that Grandfather gave up a great deal for me. He
was a virile man and, as I've said, he not
only loved women, he made love to them.
So I'm afraid that a small boy sort of
slowed him up a bit, for Grandfather had a
sense of the fitness of things and while
he wasn't ashamed of the women he loved -
and love them he did - he felt that this
was one part of his life that had no place
for a growing boy.

Of course I knew he had women friends, I
would see them on the "Twain" and I knew
that they often did stay aboard, but I
don't suppose I ever gave a thought to
where they might be sleeping at night.

It sounds strange that Mother never
learned about the "Mark Twain". Father
knew but he never questioned Grandfather
and because he was a peace-loving man who

24

wanted to avoid my mother's great rages -
one later killed her - he made sure that
she never found out.

From 1930 until 1934, "Argosy" sailed
Lake Winnipeg, the Red River, the Assini-
boine. Grandfather, Robert and I sailed
the little lifeboat to the far northern
shore of Lake Winnipeg. It was on this
cruise that I learned about the great fury
that nature can display when she throws a
tantrum. We could see the storm coming so
Grandfather took the tiller and headed the
boat to a partly sheltered little bay where
he put out three anchors and waited for the
full terror of the storm to hit.

It became as black as night so Grandfather turned on both of the electric lamps
we carried on board. The wind began to
howl and the tiny boat began to toss and
twist in the waves.

I learned the meaning of the little brass
plaque that Grandfather had mounted on the
bulkhead: "Oh God, Thy sea is so great and
my ship so small."

I wasn't afraid, though - Grandfather was
with me so God wouldn't dare hurt me ... I
was twelve. I can remember Robert sitting,
hands gripping the bunk, his face white,
and Grandfather smiling at me. Later, when
the storm was over and Grandfather and I
sat looking at the stars and Robert was
asleep in the cabin, I said, "Robert was
scared of the storm, wasn't he, Grandfather?"

Grandfather looked at me for a moment,
his voice was soft. "Yes, son, Robert was
afraid and so was I. I know that you were-
n't but that was because you are not old
enough to be really afraid yet. You see,
you take life for granted but Robert - and
me - we know that life is a gift God gives
each living creature, a gift he can and
does take back. We love life and we do
not want to lose it, not because we are

25

afraid of Death, but because we do not
want to lose life until we have fulfilled
ourselves. I know that you don't quite
understand what I've said but someday you
will." He reached over and kissed the top
of my head and I think at that moment I
knew how much that man really loved me.

The thirteenth summer of my life, 1934,
I left for England to become a deck cadet
with the British Merchant Navy. I wasn't
to remove that uniform again for fourteen
years. I was to think of that speech of
my grandfather several times during those
years ... six of them spent at war, most
of that in the Tug Rescue Service. I saw
many men die and I was close to it myself
several times and each time it wasn't
Death that frightened me but the fear that
I couldn't fulfil my life.

I didn't get back to Winnipeg until I
was sixteen. I was no longer a frightened
child but a bronzed young man in the blue
uniform of the Merchant Service. Grandfather and I sailed "Argosy" and enjoyed
living aboard the "Twain" ... Grandfather
lived aboard it full-time now. He was
fifty-one, had grown a beard, but there
wasn't a bit of grey in either his hair
or the beard. With him was a young woman.
She was, like our first maid, a long-
stemmed beauty - an Earth Mother who adored
her lover and who, when she saw that I was
a bit jealous, took me aside and told me
of how Grandfather had found her working
in a cheap cafe on Main Street in what
passed for Winnipeg's skid row. She'd
been earning seven dollars a week and working fourteen hours a day for it. She was
tired, overworked, and almost ready to
accept the offer of a pimp to work the
street. Grandfather put the pimp in the
hospital and took her under his wing.

She meekly followed him to the old river
boat and she fully expected the worst but

she was so dispirited that she didn't
really care ... she was eighteen years old
the day she met Grandfather and when she
found that he meant for her to sleep alone
and that he demanded nothing of her, at
the end of three months - it was Christmas
Eve - she went to the captain's cabin
where he slept and slipped into bed beside
him.

He was her man and she would have died
for him.

She had been with him for two years and
she was to stay with him until he went
away to war in 1939. Mother called her
Grandfather's Whore ... but never in front
of Grandfather.

When they parted, Grandfather helped her
get a job in an office. Later, when the
Canadian Women's Army Corps was formed,
she joined up, became an officer, and later
married a captain. She has two sons, one
called Peter and the other Thayne.

Today, the "Mark Twain" is no more, it
burned to the water in 1942. I now own the
land. A couple of years ago I lived in the
old house that Grandfather had moved to the
banks of the river just after the floods in
1950. In 1945, at the age of sixty-two,
Grandfather married a sixteen-year-old
Indian girl, fathered a son and a daughter.

Once more he had found a woman - for Rose
Ann was a Woman - who adored him and who
would give her life if he asked it of her.

When the war was over, I sailed a small
boat from England to the States - who did-
n't - then to Canada. I returned to Winnipeg, shipped "Argosy" to Fort William,
sailed her to Toronto by way of Fort William and the Great Lakes. After reaching
Toronto, I kept on going and sailed her to
New York. I gave "Argosy" to some American
Sea Scouts and she is still sailing on Long
Island Sound, a gallant old lady whose age
I shall never know but whose spirit is that

of a wonderful man who gave her life as he
did to people.

Peter Thayne Conroy died in 1965 at the
age of eighty-one. He had no reason to
fear Death for his life had been fulfilled
and he is one with the Gods who welcome
such as he to their company.

Our family motto is not a modest one for
it flatly states: "Only the strong deserve
God."

Grandfather was a strong man.

And so it came to pass, thirty-two years
after I had sailed my first boat, that I
once more set sail - because I wanted to
be away from the world which at times is
pretty hard for me to stand ...

CHAPTER TWO

These days there are so many rebels with
causes that they often confuse themselves,
also they have so many axes to grind that
the passer-by is often burned by flying
sparks. They howl about doing their
"thing" and they are against everything in
sight, as if they, the young of 1972, had
invented independence, freedom and the doing of one's own bloody thing.
   It is also sad to relate that these same
roaring freedom fighters become angered
and confused if one of us who dwell beyond
the gap break loose from whatever ties
bind us and start to do our own thing -
or things.
   In short, the sauce that the young goose
is enjoying should never be allowed to be
put within grabbing distance of the old
gander.
                    HAH!
   Well kiddies, here is one old gander who
has bitten off a large chunk of the cake
with the rich, creamy Independence icing
on it while he is still young enough to
enjoy it and if any of you from the far
side of the gap don't like it you may,
with my blessing, go forth and sweetly
multiply yourselves.
   The year I first tasted freedom was 1966,
I'd spent thirteen years of my life as
managing editor of a small weekly just outside of Toronto. The paper closed in the
spring of that year so I took a job in a
small town near the twin cities of Fort
William and Port Arthur (now Thunder Bay).

29

The owner of the little paper had a larger
idea then he had a bankroll so around the
middle of May I found myself with about
$120, a pet wolf, about a hundred books, a
portable TV set, a beat-up portable typewriter and some clothes - in a cheap hotel
room in Port Arthur.

I was worried because Port Arthur was
one damned lonesome place to be out of a
job in. The cost of either a bus or a
train out of there was a fair sum because
the only nearby city of any size - Canadian
city - was Winnipeg, and I knew there was
nothing in the way of jobs out there.
Leaving Belle (the wolf) in my room I went
for a walk to think things out.

I was tired, thirteen long years of
small pay, long hours and lone living was
beginning to tell on me. I needed a rest
and I needed to get away from problems
but I knew the $120 wouldn't carry me very
far so I had to come up with something
pretty fast.

Usually when I'm down in the mouth I try
to wander around a boatyard. Having owned
and loved several boats I've found that
just being around a yard filled with old
boats can perk me up no end.

There was a boatyard a few blocks away
from the hotel so I padded along the railroad tracks until I got to it. There were
a few old boats sitting on cradles and one
of them caught my eye almost the moment I
walked into the muddy yard. It was a somewhat lakeworn converted lifeboat. The
paintwork was a mess and after I climbed
up the slippery cradle to inspect the cabin
I found a musty smell and a dead cat inside where, from the look of things, no
man had set foot for some time.

There was a beat-up old Nova Scotia
"Make 'n Break" engine that looked workable and I noted that the mast, made from
a cut-down telephone pole, had a secure,

30

albeit stubby look about it. I was to
find out that the gaff-rigged sail had
been cut from - of all bloody things -
tent canvas. But from what I could see
she was free from dryrot and her small but
heavy keel was in good shape.

In short, here was a boat that was waiting for a man who loved messing about with
boats.

ME!

Blandly forgetting that I had enough
money to last me the rest of my life pro-
vided I was obliging enough to drop dead
within a half an hour, I went over to the
office to find out about my well-worn
dream boat.

The owner of the yard heard me out, then
told me the boat's history. It seemed
that a retired carpenter had built the
cabin, the lockers, bunk, table, etc.,
from good stout oak and he had used no
nails except where he'd fitted the portholes and those were brass.

He'd had a season's use, then after putting her up for the winter had sickened
and died. His son, who lived in Fort William, had no interest in the boat and had-
n't even bothered to pay the two years'
storage that was owed on it. He showed
me a rather rude reply to one of the
yard's letters about the boat.

As far as the son was concerned, the
owner of the yard could take the boat and
shove it, none of his money was going to
pay for a senile man's childish need for
a toy. The man wasn't so much interested
in the money, out of regard for his old
friend - the old man had done some carpentry work around the yard - he'd put the
boat in the water so as to keep it sweet
for the past two years but space around
the yard was getting short and he was going to handle a line of boats, he needed
all the room.

Then he offered me a deal. If - IF - I
could fit out the boat so it could be
launched within the next ten days - I
could have it for a token payment of one
nice, crisp, green, Canadian dollar bill.

I think that I got my hand into my pocket, grabbed my money, got my hand out of
my pocket, unpeeled a dollar bill and
handed it to the yard owner in all of one
second - flat out.

Leaving the grinning yard-owner to make
out a bill of sale, I dashed out of the
yard to the Salvation Army store a few
blocks away. I bought some old work
clothes and some cooking gear - I'd noticed an N.S. "fisherman's stove" in the
cabin of the boat when I'd first checked
it out - I could move aboard, cook my
meals - the stove burned wood - thereupon
saving money. Once back aboard the boat -
she now had a name, "Dulcibella" (named
after the boat in the yachting classic,
"Riddle of the Sands") - I wasted no time
in starting to work.

Now it is a fact of boating life that no
vessel can be left sitting for about two
years, wet, cold winters, wet, nasty
springs, hot summers and so-so autumns,
without having a few things get out of
shape. The companionway and the companion
slide was a bit stiff, because northwestern Ontario winters are rather messy, the
hatch or the skylight had to be kept
closed and the portholes were too small to
let in much air so the inside of the cabin
was a bit thick and musty. Several mill-
ion spiders had moved aboard and a rather
stiff cat corpse reposed in the sink. The
stove was a little rusty and the foldback
table was loaded with dusty dishes and a
number of dead insects. There was a bulkhead with a faded curtain separating the
galley and dining area from the forward
cabin where I discovered a very cosy set-

32

up. On the starboard side there was a
nice long bunk - great for someone like
myself who is tall. There was another
bunk folded into the bulkhead and I was
happy to note that mounted on the bulkhead - the one dividing the two cabins -
was a gimballed lamp. At the foot of the
bunk was a locker, and forward of that was
the head (toilet). The port side had a
small built-in desk, a closet and a set of
lockers. All of this contained in an area,
from curtain to forepeak, little more than
ten feet by five feet, six inches in size.
The after-cabin was eight feet long so I
had a living area around eighteen feet
long.

I am happy to say that by just slightly
inclining my head I had standing room. I
noted that the former owner had put in a
removable set of slat floorboards and I
was thankful that he hadn't laid either
carpet or linoleum because those two items
are just great for giving birth to little
pockets of dryrot - more so if the boat
has been laid up for a while.

Despite the dead cat, a mouldy sleeping
bag on the bunk and the dust and spiders,
I came to the conclusion that I'd bought
myself one hell of a dollar's worth of
boat.

"I had bought myself one hell of a
dollar's worth of boat."

While checking out a locker under the stove, I found four cans of unused grey marine paint. This was a saving of around thirty dollars. There was also a good American Navy peajacket in the forward cabin that a little drying out wouldn't harm and there was a good pair of seaboots skulking about in the forepeak.

There was dust everywhere. There were spiders in every nook and cranny and although I believe that old bromide - a spider living on a boat proves that the boat will never sink - I wasn't willing to allow cabin space to around 47,000 of them, but being soft-hearted I spent an hour scooping them up in an old coffee jar and putting them over the side.

I won't go into the blurred details of the next nine days except to relate that I painted, painted, scrapped, sweated, swotted, sobbed, swore and got rid of that dead cat. The yard owner set his hand to overhauling old Make 'n Break and refused to charge me one red cent for putting it in working order.

On the evening of the ninth day, supper finished and the dishes washed, I sat with my feet up on a locker and watched TV. The smoke from my pipe curled around my head, Belle, at my feet, snapped at a passing fly. I was tired but content. I felt strangely free.

I also had a plan.

Come the morrow, "Dulcibella" with her crew of two would sail towards Duluth, Sault Ste. Marie, Chicago and all lakes and waterways leading towards New York City. I'd take my time and when I ran short of money I'd write for my supper. I still had about $103 and the will to freedom.

That night as I stood in the cockpit and looked at the moon over the Sleeping Giant, I felt akin to God who must have felt the

34

same quiet contentment when he finished
making the world, for I had made my world
- a world that was thirty-six feet L.O.A.
by five feet, six inches.
    I was content.

CHAPTER THREE

It was about dawn on the tenth morning
when "Dulcibella", having been launched
late some twelve hours before, putted her
way along the Port Arthur waterfront, past
the great grain elevators and past Fort
William she chattered. There wasn't a
ghost of a breeze so old Make 'n Mend, as
I dubbed the motor, just chugged her along.
I had coffee boiling on the stove alongside of a pot of water that was boiling
two eggs as well as heating the water for
my instant porridge - thank you, Quaker
Oats, for that great way for a yachtsman
to start his day.
Belle sat with her head sticking out of
the forward hatch. She loved sailing - in
fact, she was a real Sea Wolf.
Lake Superior even on a calm day is a
tricky bitch so once in a while "Dulci"
would heel over causing me to take fast
checks on my breakfast. But she was a
good girl and left my breakfast intact.
Along about seven-thirty a light breeze
came up - from the northwest, thank God,
so up came "Dulci's" heavy beast of a
sail. The old carpenter had done a good
job of sailmaking but tent canvas is about
the worst stuff in the world to handle.
I was always damned glad that he'd made
a gaff-rigged sail so she wasn't too hard
to work. I shudder to think what I'd have
gone through if it had been the standard
sail for a thirty-six footer.
Keeping as close inshore as possible,
the stout little boat pushed her way into

the waves, the slosh-slud-slosh-slud sound
of the water breaking against her bow was
the only sound other than the creak of the
rigging and the snapping of the Red Duster
flying from the jack-staff. The sun was
bright but there was a chill in the air so
I made sure that there was always a hot
cup of good, sweet boaty tea ready for me.

Which brings me to a pause in my story
so that I can explain how boaty tea is
made.

First you go to a Salvation Army store
and you buy a large enamel tea pot - the
kind they use in lumber camps or skidrow
missions - after scouring it with boiling
water, you throw in about four handfuls of
tea. You boil the tea, drink it - adding
plenty of sugar - then you put the teapot
at the back of your stove.

The next time you want a cup, you add
more tea leaves BUT YOU NEVER THROW OUT

"There was always a hot cup of
good, sweet, boaty tea."

37

THE OLD LEAVES - YOU JUST KEEP ADDING TO
WHAT HAS BEEN USED BEFORE.

The result is a strong cup of what British yachtsmen call "boaty tea", a drink
that was created for strong men whose
interests are boating and women.

Somehow, I have never been able to interest my shore-bound friends in making it,
much less drinking it.

Meanwhile, back on the lake. There was-
n't much of a wind so "Dulci" just plodded
along, never making more than around three
knots, which if she kept going at her pres-
ent rate of speed would get her to the U.S.
border at Pigeon River within about twelve
hours. I wasn't sure of the hours that
the Americans kept - some border crossing
points are a pain in the stern to a yachtsman - so I hoped I'd arrive before they
closed for the night.

I needn't have worried, Grand Portage is
open all the time. Besides, by the time
I got there I was pretty tired and Belle
needed a run ashore so I tied up at a dock
for the night. Except for the sound of
the great trucks bashing their way into
the U.S. or Canada, Grand Portage folds up
at night. On the Canadian side at Pigeon
River there is a motel and a restaurant
but I couldn't go back and forth so I
stayed put, made supper, fed Belle, did
the dishes, propped myself up against the
bulkhead and watched TV.

When the dawn came up like soft thunder,
we were away towards Duluth which sat
smoking and dirty eighty-odd miles away.

There is not much of anything except
wilderness between Thunder Bay and Duluth.
There are three small towns, little more
than a number of bars and gas stations,
and the shoreline is dotted with a few
summer camps as they call their cottages
in that area.

It is no place for the tyro to take his

"Getting caught out on Lake Superior
is a pretty dangerous game to play."

boat because Lake Superior is dangerous
and many a life has been lost when the Big
S has had a blow.
  Added to the problem of fast storms and
unannounced blows, the shoreline of Minnesota is pretty straight, there aren't too
many sheltered bays so getting caught out
on Lake Superior is a pretty dangerous
game to play. In point of fact, I was
held up in Two Harbors for two days while
all hell broke loose. The pitching and
tossing of my little boat caused me to
feel the first touch of sea-sickness I'd
suffered in twenty years - and I was moored to a dock at the time.
  All in all, it took me well over a week
to get to Duluth. Not being a member of
any yacht club, I was unable to stay at
the club's moorings, but there was a
friendly marina nearby and as he charged

only 12¢ a foot per day for mooring and he even had a grocery counter, I was better off in the long run.

I stayed in Duluth for a week for although "Dulci" was a good boat, her shakedown cruise had shown me that there were a few things to be done. The icebox, always a source of trouble on a small boat, was leaking. Using charcoal in my stove was a dirty pain in the neck, so I stocked up with a sack of coal. I also needed a larger container for my kerosene - this was for my lamps and the gimballed stove that was used when it was too hot to use the fisherman's stove.

I also found a small leak in the deckhead - neatly situated right over my head when I climbed into my bunk.

I don't know what Duluth is like now but five years ago it was a dirty city with one of the biggest bookstores in the midwestern United States.

My next major stop was to be Sault Ste. Marie so when I readied "Dulcibella" for her next run along the northern shores of two and a quarter states - Minnesota, Wisconsin and Michigan - I wondered how many other men had sailed small boats along my route.

I was to find out that not any had tried it single-handed except a couple of guys with canoes.

I spent almost a week gunk-holing around the Apostle Islands. There were a few camps on these islands but it was a little early in the season for the Americans - here in Canada, our open-the-summer-cottage time is the twenty-fourth of May. With the Americans, it seems they wait until the fourth of July.

Belle spent a lot of time stalking squirrels but never catching them - I always made sure the area was really deserted because I didn't want some trigger-happy nit with a gun popping off at her.

40

"Dulci" would be anchored off-shore -
the dink, loaded with food, tea, beer,
radio, books, painting gear, wolf and just
room enough for me, would be paddled
ahore for long hot days on the beach - and
never another human in sight. As a matter
of fact, the only people I saw for six
days were on the screen of my little Sony
TV.

I was damned glad that I had the wood
stove on board "Dulcibella" because the
nights were still chilly and a fire in
its small belly made for a nice cosy cabin
after dark.

As a matter of fact, the nights were
pretty chilly until I got around to Lake
Huron in July.

Between the Apostle Islands and Copper
Harbor there is only one real port, Onton-
agon, and it is much like countless small
towns in that part of the States. Shabby
houses, dirty streets and more taverns per
square foot then there are schools or lib-
raries in the whole damn state - not that
it would really matter about the town having a library anyway because the types who
live in these towns are no different than
the union-men-working-stiffs either in
Canada or the U.S. - great hulking lumps
whose idea of a big night is sitting slop-
ping down cheap hooch or gallons of beer
while watching some sport on a TV set - I
will admit here and now that I am a happy
snob and the less I have to do with the
lower classes - be they white, black or
pink-bloody-polkadot - the better I like
it.

I hadn't been on the main street of the
town more than four minutes when some
idiot tried to pick a fight with me because of my beard. As luck would have it,
there was a U.S. Coast Guard vessel in
port and some of the hands sided in with
me, because after I'd belted the knothead
some of his buddies tried to jump me.

41

I spent the remainder of my evening on board the C.G. cutter and left early the next morning.

But let me be honest about it, I get caught up in these hassles because I usually walk around with an expression on my face that rather points out that I've just finished eating my young so I can't really blame some guy for wanting to part my beard with his fist.

I am a wee bit of a curmudgeon, a non-social animal in a world filled with organized togetherness. I never sit in bars, beer parlors or night clubs. I belong to one club, one of those large stone heaps with a good library, working fireplaces, excellent port, deep leather chairs and members who'd cut you dead if you speak more than three words.

As a slight concession to the seventies, they have allotted what used to be the second bridge room to those who watch TV. I find that there are only three of us who use it - even on Hockey Night in Canada nights.

There are also a few monk-like cells for those of us who needs must take shelter for the night. Like the ex-colonel who, because his wife's funeral had been held late in the afternoon, stayed over because "that damned traffic to the suburbs would make drivin' to me place in the country a bloody bore."

It isn't that I dislike people, I just can't stand overwhelming crowds of them. I think it stems from having been - from the age of thirteen until I was twenty-seven - first a cadet, then an officer in the British Merchant Navy. I spent fifteen years of my life crowded into small ships and tugs with oodles of people.

There is bound to be some sort of reaction.

I do like young women though.

Hell! I'm normal.

CHAPTER FOUR

If you are to make a lifetime habit of
single-handed cruising, it's best that you
have no shore-bound home, job, wife or con-
science, or if you do take onto yourself a
mate, better it be a mistress, for at
least then the poor girl will have an
easier route of escape than if she were
tied down by a marriage licence.

Life aboard a small boat isn't all sun-
lit skies, quiet bays and beautiful independence. It's rain-drenched cockpits, a
cooking fire that won't start, pumping out
the remains of the last storm, being held
up in some dismal lake port because all
hell is blowing up a gale. It's all of
this and sometimes a bit more but I would-
n't want to live any other way.

A cynic may ask, "OK, brother, if you're
so all-fired set on a life of adventure,
why stick to the lakes and canals? Why
not go to sea and have real adventure?"

I have no ambition to sail a small boat
to windward against South Atlantic gales,
rolling horribly, oft-times being seasick
almost to death. Being always wet, filled
with apprehension and very often terrified.

Away back in 1946 I did just that - when
I sighted the West Indies through red-
rimmed eyes, I croaked out of a throat raw
from rancid water, "This is it - I'm
through."

To me, there is real adventure in dis-
covering a small port in a quiet backwater
in Georgian Bay. To sail inshore near a
highway and watch the lights from speeding

43

automobiles swishing along at seventy per
and know that they will never hear the cry
of a night bird, be startled by the sudden
splash made by a fish jumping out of the
water close to the hull. When they at
last stop for the night, it will be in a
motel room, sterile, cold, looking like
countless other rooms along some ribbon of
concrete, whereas I'll anchor in some
little bay, sit snug in my great sweater,
mug of tea in my hand, pipe glowing in the
dark, restfully tired, not bone weary from
long hours of sitting hunched behind the
wheel and never seeing the passing hills,
the clouds, or feel the gentle wind
against the cheek.

However, I won't say that I was sorry to
sight the smoke-ringed skyline of the two
Sault Ste. Maries.

Here and now, I take a stand. This book
will contain no long-winded descriptions
of passing through locks, breathtaking
natterings about towering walls and rush-
ing waters so beloved of most people who
write for yachting magazines. Suffice to
say I got from Lake Superior to Lake Huron.

Locking through may be fun and games for
some people but it's a great fat pain in
the stern for me.

For this reason, I have avoided the dub-
ious joys of the Rideau and Trent canals
although I do like locking along the Erie
Canal because this one can do without the
fuss and feathering of motor that the two
Canadian waterways force on one.

I was planning to continue to swing west
towards Lake Michigan and Chicago ...

Wisconsin, a little of Illinois and Indiana, and a great deal of Michigan surround
Lake Michigan. It is a busy lake and if
one wishes - and has the time - after
reaching the Windy City, he can follow the
Chicago Ship Canal to the Mississippi,
then after a short run turn north and

cruise to Minneapolis and St. Paul.

I must do that some day.

Sailing under the great bridge that spans the Mackinaw Straits is an awesome experience and I suppose I did what everybody who goes under that great span does - I took pictures and shot movies, tacking back and forth several times so as to get good shots. After spending several days meandering along the north shore I discovered that food was running low - plenty of Alpo but Belle resented anyone eating her food, so I set my course for a town called Escanaba.

And therein hangs a tale.

Her name was Daisy, she was a bar girl in one of the town's many taverns. Just twenty-two, she left school at fifteen to find a life in a town.

She worked as a waitress in a series of one-armed joints, married a seaman from one of the lakeboats when she was eighteen and landed a job in this bar when she was twenty-one. I was something new in her life. She'd never met a writer before and she thought that the only people who lived on boats were men like her now ex-husband who worked on the big lakers.

The first night in town I went to the local movie house and after the show was over, feeling like a beer, picked out the joint with the least people and a silent jukebox in it.

It wasn't as dark as some of these places usually are, so choosing a table as far from the noise-box as possible I waited on. I didn't have too long to wait. She came over to the table, order-book in hand, smile on her face and wearing an outfit that proved beyond any shadow of any doubt whatsoever that she was all girl.

Long beautiful legs up to the shoulders, small waist, big healthy breasts, she stirred a memory or two in me.

45

I ordered a beer and a beef sandwich and watched her walk away. When she came back to the table, she stayed to talk.

The owner of the place, a fat Greek who looked like he'd been born out of the grease he cooked his food on, encouraged his two bar girls to be friendly to the customers on slow nights. I knew the drill but this girl was somewhat awed by me. I was different than the miners and farmers who usually came in to drink and watch the fights on TV. I read books, I didn't talk like the people she'd known all her life and I didn't keep looking down her open blouse all the time.

To be honest about it, I nursed a hope or two. After all, single-handed sailing is fun but single-handed sleeping can be a damn bore.

I bought a beer for the people in the room - six of them - and a shot for the slob who owned the joint. About one in the morning the place closed, I'd already asked Daisy if I could take her home - by this time I knew that she lived alone in a cheap hotel not far from the bar - she'd said yes ... she told me later that the greaseball had told her to.

She just threw a coat over her skimpy costume and tucked her arm in mine, we said goodnight to the gentleman from the land of that other great Greek, Onassis.

Somehow, after we got outside, I didn't want to go to her hotel - it would have been like mucking about with a whore and Daisy wasn't that. I suggested that we go down to my boat, it was docked only a block away at an old concrete pier. She agreed.

When she saw "Dulcibella", she purred like a kitten and while I winced a bit at the use of the word "cute" when applied to my boat, I accepted it for what it was, a compliment.

She took to Belle right off and to my
surprise Belle even licked her cheek.
Belle didn't usually take to people right
off - she was a one-man animal - but I was
to find that this simple girl had a heart
filled with love for everything.

She was a healthy young animal who liked
making love because it was the most friendly thing that two people could share.

A rather basic philosophy but one I am
inclined to agree with.

We sat, drank coffee, talked and then
made love. There was no tricks, no feeling that she'd read all the books - the
how-to books - that turn love-making into
a ritual that is merely erotic rather than
joyful.

She only wanted to give pleasure and did.

I was touched by her getting up the next
morning and making breakfast. I even got
mine served to me in my bunk.

She didn't have to be at work until
around six o'clock so we spent the next
day together. We shopped for food, visited the local war surplus store and made
plans to leave Escanaba together.

She was tired of her job and she'd been
planning to go to Chicago for a long time,
and when she found out I was set to cruise
in that direction, she asked me if I'd
take her.

It would be easy. That night, a Friday,
was pay-night for her, she'd collect it,
pick up her small amount of belongings and
off we'd go.

Everything went as planned. I left the
boat around twelve-thirty, went to the bar,
had a couple of beers, and when the place
closed we said goodnight to the greaseball
and within fifteen minutes "Dulci" was cut-
ting across Green Bay with the pair of us
giggling like naughty children who are
playing hookey from school.

I might add that she left a note for her

47

boss stuck in the mailslot - I hope he was able to find someone to read it to him.

We took our time sailing to Chicago. Long days were spent with her sunbathing until her deep tan set off her blonde hair to shining like spun gold.

As the Quakers are wont to say, she pleasured me.

Then I began to worry about Chicago. It, like most big cities, is a damn jungle and it bothered me that I was supposed to leave her there.

I really liked her, she was sweet, gentle and we'd had good times together. I didn't want her to end up working in some hole where anything could happen to her.

As we neared Chicago, a plan formed in my mind. I'd take her to Detroit, arrange for her to take a business course and in that way I'd be sure that she'd be safe and secure.

When I outlined my plan to her she burst into tears, for the nearer to Chicago we got, the more afraid she'd become.

She was easy to understand. To her, working and living in small towns all her life, Chicago was a dream, an escape hatch. Like the planters in the Burmese jungles who always plan to go home but never do, she too had dreamed her dream and on impulse she'd asked me to take her away - she never dreamed that I'd really go along with the idea.

But she did want to see Chicago so we sailed on, gunk-holing into little creeks, walking the beaches and drinking great steins of Milwaukee beer.

The Windy City was now just a short way from "Dulci's" bow.

CHAPTER FIVE

A great many things may be said against
Chicago. A police force largely made up
of hardheads, mayors who consort with gang-
sters. There is also a feeling about the
people of Chicago that they live in a world
apart. They call their city "Chicago-land"
and it was there that I saw a great bloody
sign with the words, "THE FAMILY THAT SHOPS
TOGETHER - STAYS TOGETHER!" emblazoned
across the side of a large building.

But whatever else may be wrong with it,
at least some early city fathers were able
to save most of its long waterfront. There
are miles of beaches, yacht clubs and marinas along Chicago's shoreline. They are
well-kept and patrolled at all times.

There is also a strong anti-British -
this includes Canadians - outlook in Chicago. As a matter of fact, back forty
years ago, Mayor "Big Bill" Thompson,
friend of Capone and "Bugs" Moran, helped
himself win another election by promising
the voters - those solid-headed Germans
and hunkies who sweated away their beer by
working in the stockyards and steel mills
- that, if elected, "I'll go over to England and punch King George in the nose."
Of course he was helped by having the vot-
ing power of the sort of Shanty Irish that
my great-grandfather whipped out of their
sordid huts during the great famine and
whom my grandfather sent packing when they
came to him for jobs during the depression.

We Irish have never been too nice to
other Irish.

But Daisy wanted to see the place and I was agreeable so we tied up at dock in the Chicago River. Where we tied up was close to the Loop - the Chicago Tribune building was our neighbour. We could have moored at the lakefront but I wanted us to be nearer the heart of the city.

It was late in the afternoon when we tied up so Daisy got dinner ready while I did some cleaning up around the boat. As I puttered, I came up with an idea. We'd spend the night in a hotel. A room in a hotel - baths in real tubs. Wide beds. Room service. "Dulcibella" would be safe at her dock, the only way down to her was through a gate and there was a watchman in a little hut and a great, high electric fence all around the place. Besides, Belle was on guard.

Daisy was charmed by the idea and after dinner and dishes were finished off she put on her nice new dress - I'd picked it out in Milwaukee - put her golden hair into the braids I liked and gave me a kiss.

Me, I just climbed into my usual turtle-neck sweater, my old reefer, put on my shore-going hat, picked up our small suit-case and we were off.

Stopping at the watchman's hut, I phoned the Chicago-Hilton and reserved a room - with bath. I explained that we were sailing a small boat to Chicago and would be a little late - around 10:30 - before we'd check in.

I reserved the room for Mr. and Mrs. Conroy. Daisy giggled.

We wandered around the Loop a bit, took in a movie and then had one of those vast steaks which made Chicago a great place to visit. It was around eleven when we reached our hotel. Not a flicker crossed the clerk's face as he surveyed my salty garb and beard that needed kempting. With an "Enjoy your stay in Chicago" he passed us

over to a bellboy who picked up our bag
and whipped us into an elevator run by a
very pretty Negro girl, to our fifteenth-
floor room.

After ridding ourselves of him with a
small tip, we collapsed on the bed laugh-
ing.

I sat watching Johnny Carson while Daisy
soaked in the tub, as a matter of fact I
was well into the late, late show when she
- at last - came over to my chair, shining
and warm.

I sat and soaked, watched the movie -
Daisy had wheeled the colour set near the
door of the bathroom - for almost an hour,
then out to lie face down on the bed while
Daisy gave me a rubdown that sent tingles
all up and down my id.

We sat watching the movie together for
a while, then Daisy tumbled into bed. I
watched until the last Indian bit the
dust, then I too turned towards the bed.

The bed lamp was still turned on - it
was one of those with a dimmer - it softly glowed on the still form of the girl.
Its glimmer brought out the gold of her
hair, she lay curled up like a little
girl, one shoulder strap had slipped down,
one perfect breast was bared. She looked adorable and I was glad that I'd
brought her along. Not because she was
good in bed because that kind of relationship wouldn't have lasted sixty miles.

No, there was something more. It wasn't
love, we were fond of each other and we
enjoyed our time spent together but we
were not in love.

If we had been in love, Daisy wouldn't
have taken the pill - it was as simple as
that.

She had a bright mind, she was beginning
to both read and understand my books. She
was a warm, sweet human who I hoped would
be able to find a decent man, have his

51

babies and live in a nice house.

She had a nice voice - not the nasty
nasal twang one finds in all too many American girls. I got her out of a nasty American - and Canadian - habit, chewing gum.
Her way of make-up was toned down. I recall that as we walked through the hotel
she looked better than any of the sleek
young women who were in the lobby.

My playing a sea-going Professor Higgins
to her American Midwest Elisa was paying
off.

I slipped into bed beside her, leaned
over, kissed her gentle cheek, and slid
down under the covers.

And fell to sleep a happy man.

CHAPTER SIX

The next morning, our living the way the
other half did being at an end, we returned to "Dulci" and the planning of our day.
Daisy wanted to visit a business school to
find out about courses and I wanted to
take a manuscript over to "Playboy", so
off we went on our separate errands.

When we met again at noon I had good
news, "Playboy" had accepted my story, but
Daisy was one shaken-up young girl. It
seemed that, having left school in grade
eight, no business school would accept her
- at least that is what she'd been told by
the people at the school where she'd spent
an ego-busting morning.

She also told me that she wanted to remain in Chicago, that, while she enjoyed
being with me and cruising on the lakes,
she wanted to find a job - she could always go back to being a cocktail waitress
- and forget dreams of glory.

In a way it was my fault because I'd
built her up and had raised her hopes
without thinking about the way the world
operates. I asked her to give me a couple
of days more to work something out because
I just couldn't see her working in one of
the swarmy joints having to be nice to a
lot of slavering slobs.

Daisy wasn't the kind of girl to sit
around feeling sorry for herself, she soon
bounced back to being her usual cheerful
self, but I could sense her disappointment
at the way the people at the school had
treated her.

It always bothers me when I see someone who has intelligence, talent and drive being put down because they've missed a few years of school or have the wrong kind of name. I'll admit too that my ego had taken a bit of a bruising for the new Daisy was my creation. I had, within a few short weeks - having a very bright and willing pupil - been able to take a pretty but crude young girl and turn her into a poised and charming young woman. The school's rejection of Daisy was my rejection too.

I fell back on a ploy that had worked in the past. When you come up against a wall that won't give, you use the power of the press to bulldoze your way through. I had such a wedge to use for Daisy.

An old friend worked on one of the Chicago papers. One of its editors, he had some influence and like myself he had a dislike of walls. A phone call, a few words and Daisy and I were on our way to have lunch with him.

From the moment we met in front of the restaurant - a good one with soft-footed waiters, gleaming tablecloths and a wine list - I could see him watching her, for to be turned loose in one of these places is a test in itself.

Daisy passed with flying colours. She was poised, well-groomed, beautiful, and she was to the manner born. I was proud of her. She was honest about her past and her relationship with me. She told him about how I'd made her feel important and how she wanted something better than the prospect of ending her days either working as a middle-aged waitress in some cheap cafe or being married to some part-time slob with grimy hands and no education.

Bob liked her, and he opened up a new avenue of career. His wife was a model -

54

a high-priced model - so he knew girls who, though they lacked formal schooling, had made it as models. He excused himself and went to phone his wife.

When he returned he had a smile on his face, his wife wanted to meet Daisy so we were invited to their lakeshore apartment for dinner that evening. The cool, poised young woman became the impulsive child-woman again. She threw her arms around Bob and kissed him.

Bob didn't look too unhappy about it.

After leaving Bob at the door to the paper I grabbed Daisy by the hand and we started running towards the Loop. I wanted to buy her a whole new outfit - "Play-boy" pays well - so we were on our way to a little shop where Daisy had seen a dress she liked. She had innate good taste so I was going to let her choose for herself and I wasn't too surprised when she stopped at a newsstand on the way and bought a fashion magazine.

When we reached the shop I became extra baggage while she and the pretty manager poured over the magazine, chattered, eye-boggled and purred their way through a world that I'd have been lost in.

Daisy went the whole route, from sexy but tasteful underthings to a dress that almost knocked my eyes out. When she stood in front of me, tall and proud in her new finery, I knew that she would never again be forced to work like a part-time bawd in some rancid hole for the benefit of blubbery clowns who had the desire but not the ability to bed her.

Dinner that night was a roaring success. Both Bob and Anna took to her and it was Anna who came up with a great idea. She'd been forced to cut down on her modeling because of the baby - help was hard to find - so she proposed that, if Daisy were willing, she could live with them. look

after the baby, and they would pay her way
through modeling school and Anna would
help her find assignments. Daisy looked
at me, eyes shining; I grinned at her and
said yes.

They arranged that Daisy would move in
at the end of the week. I was happy about
this, for it would give us a few more days
together. That night aboard "Dulcibella"
Daisy clung to me like a child, she was
happy but she was a little fearful because
we were to part in a few short days. I'd
been a sort of father-lover to her. She
trusted me and she was grateful to me for
what had happened.

How did I feel! I'd miss her but I knew
it was best for her. Sure, we'd had fun
together, we had laughed, made love, walked and shared things. She had given me of
herself and for the first time in years I
had given myself.

I'll admit that I spent a few moments
standing on the dock, looking down at
Daisy sitting reading on the foredeck, and
feeling damned sorry for myself.

The three days till Friday passed too
fast but we had a ball. We enjoyed.

Then came the parting. I took her to
the lakeshore apartment and Anna under-
standingly left us alone for a few moments.
We both cried a little and then as I left
Anna and Daisy told me they would hang a
bright red blanket on the balcony rail so
I could see them through the glasses as
they watched me sail by. I said I'd phone
just before I cast off so they'd get
plenty of warning.

It meant sailing a bit northward so I
hoped the wind would be right - from the
south.

About an hour later, as the dinner-hour
traffic sped along the lakeshore, I jibed
my way inshore so that the two girls could
see me. I held the glasses to my somewhat

56

blurred eyes and I could just make them
out some sixteen floors above the street,
waving.

I came about and sailed a sad course
that would take me northward along the
western shore of Michigan. I hugged Belle
to me, and taking one last look at the
fast-disappearing tower where my little
friend was to build a future, I turned my
face towards the smokestack of Gary,
Indiana.

And cried like hell.

CHAPTER SEVEN

Later that night as I sat in my snug
little cabin, drawing on a good cigar,
sipping my beer and watching a good movie
on TV, I reflected - during the commercials - that I had a good life. My small
home could take me anywhere I chose to
go. I ate well, slept well, was a free
man, I owned everything I ate off, drank
from and slept under - which is more than
most people could say.

I could, if I so chose, even have someone to share my life. I took a long draw
on my cigar, sighed, and mentally snapped
my fingers at the world.

I was feeling pretty damn smug.

After the movie was finished, I wrote to
Daisy, then went ashore to post the letter.
It was about three in the morning, the
streets were deserted and there was a bit
of fog. I strolled along, snug in my peajacket, old M.N. cap tilted over my eyes,
puffing my favourite pipe. I felt good.

Something had to happen.

It did. A patrol car pulled over to the
curb ahead of me. One very large Mackinaw
City cop unfolded from the car.

"You live around here?"

"No, I'm from Canada."

"Stayin' at a hotel?"

"No, I'm ..."

"Oh. Where's your car parked?"

"I don't have a car, I came here in my
boat ... from Fort William."

"Where is this boat at?"

"It's down at an old dock at the foot of
this street."

58

They made me get in the car, and when we got to the dock and out of the car, one cop moved along on either side of me. When we reached "Dulcibella" the second cop spoke for the first time. He pointed to Belle, who was tied up in the cockpit. "Look at the size of that gawdamned thing, Harry."

Harry peered at her, his flashlight on her head. Now, Belle's eyes shone a bright red in the dark when a light, even from the moon, reflected in them.

"Jesus, that thing has got wolf in it."

I told a slight lie, I said Belle was a Canadian Eskimo dog that was part wolf. While all this was going on, Belle just lay quietly on her blanket. But Belle was a bloody ham and if she knew she was the centre of attention she howled with pleasure.

She howled and thereupon scared the be-jabbers out of both cops.

The result was that I was told to get the hell out of Mackinaw City – right then – right away or dire things would happen to both me and my animal. The cops waited until my boat moved away from the shore.

Later, at Harbor Beach, the Michigan State Police told me that those cops had no legal right to do what they did but I reasoned that if I made waves, they'd make waves, so to hell with it, the incident was closed.

Lake Huron, like Lake Superior, is a big boat lake and the early July weather was perfect. Balmy winds made sailing a pleasure and while I couldn't move as swiftly as the bigger sailboats, mostly American, I wouldn't have traded in "Dulci" for six of them.

I just lazed along, spending a couple of days here, a few hours there. And as I barged along it came to me that there were

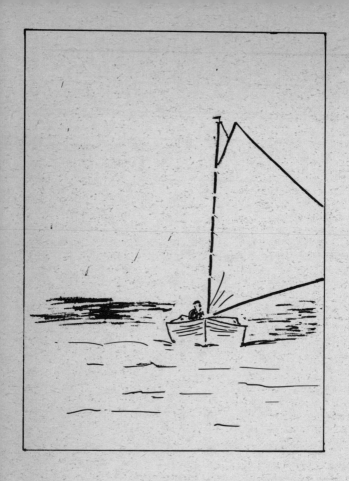

"Balmy winds made sailing a pleasure
-- I just lazed along."

more of my kind in England than in either
Canada or the States. The single-handed
sailors, the messers-about with boats, the
happy breed.

I preferred little docks or old unused
piers to mooring in boatyards or yacht
clubs. I was happier remaining aboard
my boat, writing, reading or watching TV,
than sitting in some bar or yacht club
lounge. When I did go ashore it was to
walk Belle, buy supplies, or go to a show.

Unless it could be with someone like
Daisy, I would rather sail alone. I suppose it was spending fifteen years of living among Englishmen that did it.

As I said before, the English have this
trait that makes them like puttering
about in small boats in godawful weather,
go cruising during the winter months, and
then, after years of living in some comfortable, riverside house within commut-
ing distance of London - and with a position in "the City" - retire to live aboard
some converted lifeboat or small cruiser
called "Water Gypsy", "Wild Love" or even
"Sea Fury".

Every day of the year except on Hols
you'd see them, catching the 8:10 for the
City, dark grey trousers, black coat,
bowler and furled brolly, brief case and
morning paper, walking to the station. The
very picture of the proper middle-class
Englishman. Cool, intolerant of all that
isn't English but willing to give his life
for the non-English, he is the model for
everything that is establishment, for all
the world to wonder at ... beside him the
American in the grey flannel suit is a
pallid imitation.

But on the weekends you'll find him wearing clothes that a bagman would scorn as
rags, a beat-up sailor's cap on his head,
a cold wind biting at his guts, there he
sits at the tiller of "Gypsy", a cup of
tea in his gloved fist, a foul pipe in his

mouth and a happy soul.

I'm proud to be one of the breed.

Except for the very few - the late Robert Maury who sailed the twelve-foot "Tinker Belle" from the states to England was one of them - there are not too many single-handed lone-wolf sailors either in Canada or the U.S. I think it is because we North Americans have an inbred fear of being alone. We have always mistrusted the loner. Newspapers always make much of the criminal who is "reported to be a man who lived alone and who had no close friends ..."

We are joiners, groupies who flock together like scared birds, almost frightened if we aren't within the sound of a human voice. We have to have sound around us - look at the way our stores and streets in the business sections scream with loud, nasty music. How, no matter what they're doing, the young have to have a damn transistor radio going ... I even got behind a couple in a movie one night who were playing one WHILE THE BLOODY MOVIE was on. They skawed about their "rights" when I demanded that they shut it off.

We huddle together in great cities, yet we hide behind barred doors. We must live in groups but we refuse to become involved too much with the group. If a child at summer camp wants to go for a walk by himself, some nit who once read a book writes a report, "James is somewhat anti-social and is not group-orientated."

Great Christ in the boondocks!

All that because some normal eleven-year-old wants to go for a walk in the woods - by himself.

But we who go down to the rivers, the lakes, the canals, we endure being cold and wet. While we are weekend cruising, meals are ignored - we snatch something from out of a can, cold - drink gallons of

strong tea. Often we live in damp cloth-
ing for days on end and somehow we never
catch anything - but let one of us have to
wait ten minutes for a bus in the rain and
we spend a month in bed with a hot water
bottle.

We are intolerant of the joys of others,
firmly believing that the fellow who goes
golfing in October is quite mad, while we,
who have just completed a round-trip
cruise of eighty miles in an early snow
storm, are really quite sane.

Of our boats we are proud, be it fifty-
three feet of grandeur at eight thousand
dollars a foot or a beat-up old tub we
purchased for three hundred, complete with
trailer.

In short, you may rape our wives, insult
our mothers, call us bastards and what-
have-you, but don't insult our dockside
pride and joy.

Those of us who mess about with boats
are truly touched with madness ... and we
wouldn't have it any other way.

CHAPTER EIGHT

For the first day or so after leaving Chicago I missed Daisy, but by the time
"Dulci" reached Muskegon - port for the
ferry from Milwaukee - I was well back into single-handed sailing and, I'm afraid,
well recovered from having to face cruising alone. I'm afraid that most writers
- and many artists - are like that, somewhat curmudgeon in habit and loners by
choice.

As I wrote in another chapter, no woman
in her right mind should marry one of us.

As "Dulci" barged along like a pregnant
walrus, I puttered about, fixing this,
breaking that, and eating a stew that
never seemed to grow less with the passing of the days - I think the damn thing
procreated itself while it sat in the dark
icebox. It lasted until I reached Mackinaw City - a nice little town that strad-
dles both Lake Michigan and Lake Huron -
then I tossed what was left to the fish.
Belle wouldn't touch it, she, furry fuss-
pot that she was, just sniffed at it and
snorted.

As I say, I puttered, and a putter is
the best I can do when it comes to being
a handyman. I'm no bloody expert and I'm
glad. Experts are never happy, they are
always trying to improve on everything.
Me, I'm happy - and grateful that anything
works at all.

Funny thing is, I always seem to win out.
For example, in Montreal I lived in a house
with a TV set and no antenna on the roof.

I was told by experts that, without either cable TV or all that plumbing on the roof, I couldn't get Channel 5, a nearby Vermont station. Not being an expert, I plunged onward where angels and TV repairmen feared to wire. I strung a long loop of antenna wire to a beat-up, bent-wire coathanger and hung it near the window - and BONG-BONG-Dong! - I got good old NBC and the Johnny Carson show.

Of course, it was a little hazy but what the hell, on $27 worth of TV set I'm expecting maybe living colour?

That is one reason why I won't have an outboard motor on any boat of mine except the little British Seagull. THAT motor was designed for the guy like me, the guy who can mess up lowering a window blind.

As a matter of fact, in his wonderful book about the St. Pierre dory, "Billy Ruffian, the Thousand Dollar Yacht", Anthony Bailey tells about one of these little workhorses that spent a day and a half submerged in salt water and was Lazarus-like restored to life by a bit of cleaning and a lot of love. The sturdy little Seagull is as simple for the non-expert to do simple repairs on as was the old Model-T engine.

And he only paid twenty-five bucks for it too.

We puttered on, northwards to Detroit. It suddenly came to me that I'd been mucking about for almost two months and I hadn't touched Canadian waters once. At the risk of seeming to be disloyal to Canada, I prefer it that way. Canadian waters may be fun for Americans to cruise about in, but for a Canadian they're a pain in the bloody stern. The little ports that dot Ontario - which has ninety-eight percent of the cruising waters for small boat owners in Eastern (Ontario-Quebec) Canada - usually make Canadian SMALL boat owners feel like bums or people to be rooked.

I remember once looking for mooring or dock space at a Canadian marina. I was shoved into a spot near a sewer outlet. I noted some open moorings and docking spaces. When I asked why I wasn't put at one of those, I was blandly told - with a sniff of contempt for "Dulcibella" - that they were for American boats, and besides, Canadians didn't want to spend money.

Being me, I demanded my money back, got it, and shoved off to dock at a government dock. It was better in the long run. It was closer to the centre of the town and besides, it was free.

Now, this isn't the fault of the Americans. The American yachtsman as a whole is a gentleman and like his Canadian counterpart he would be willing to accept the bad with the good.

And here too I am afraid I prefer the American marina operators to most of the defrocked used-car salesmen who prey on their fellow Canadians.

A sure way of knowing that you are going to get a decent break in Canada is to go to a line yard that has been in business for at least twenty years and usually calls itself a "boat yard" rather than a marina. I might add that here in Canada the word "marina" means damn all, for a good many of these so-called marinas are located miles from water and sell overpriced fibreglass runabouts to idiots, while in the States a marina means just that, a place where boats are sold, stored, and serviced at a location on the water.

An example of a good boat yard is the Metro Marine in Bronte, Ontario. This yard, in business since 1921, is one of the best.

The man in charge, Ivan Snyder, sold me a boat in June 1972 for the cost of stor-

66

age owing, and gave me several cans of
paint. His son John put the old 1932
Buick motor (converted to marine use) in
shape and all I was charged was $40 plus
the cost of a six-volt battery.

Knowing the state of my bank account,
they didn't charge me anything while I
worked on "Dulcibella II" and let me
scrounge good gear off a couple of old
abandoned boats.

They are typical of the kind of men -
all too few - who know how to operate a
boat yard.

If I sound nasty, I mean to. Any clown
with an itch to make money can sell boats
in this country. He doesn't have to know
a damn thing about boats and he usually
doesn't. All too often he sells too much
motor for too little boat. He never bothers to pick up a copy of that little bull-
etin on safe boating that is issued yearly
by the Department of Transport and he
never advises anyone to get his boat lic-
ensed.

In short, the average fat-cat boat dealer who parks his wares on the side of a
highway far, far from lakes or rivers is
a buck-hungry slob who should be pushed
out of the business.

Because he sure as hell isn't doing the
Canadian boating industry any good.

There, I've gotten that off my chest, I
can get on with the book.

I gunk-holed and ghosted along, never in
a hurry, for hurrying was something I was-
n't interested in doing. I had a small
plan - once I reached Detroit, I'd rest up
for a few days, maybe I'd even favour
Windsor with a visit although I've always
felt that it was a poor relation of Detroit. As a matter of fact, I didn't plan
on going into Canada at all because my
route was clearly in American waters all
the way to New York City - but later I

67

planned, when I reached Buffalo, to catch
a train for Toronto where I was to sell
an article about my trip. Let's face it,
I may not like cruising in Canadian waters
too much but I'm not against picking up
some Canadian money so I can continue
cruising in the U.S.

When I reached Mackinaw City there was
a letter waiting for me from Daisy. She
was happy and she was grateful for what
had happened and she loved my friends. I
sighed a little for my lost light-of-love
and went to a Randolph Scott movie.

CHAPTER NINE

Detroit in the early summer of 1966 was
still a city where a man could walk the
downtown streets in safety and because I
like - or rather, used to like - the place,
I rather enjoyed my short stay there. I
moored "Dulci" at an unused portion of an
excursion dock, spent my days writing an
article for the Free Press and my evenings
either going to movies or watching TV.

Not an exciting life, but then no matter
what we do I suppose it becomes a matter
of routine. A soldier of fortune isn't
always up-ending a bottle or a broad, he
has orderly room duties to do. A Mafia
killer has to make out expense account
reports and an explorer has to worry about
keeping to schedule.

I remember standing in envy of my cap-
tains when I first went into the Merchant
Navy as a junior officer. I pictured a
captain as a great awesome figure who
stood on the bridge barking out terse orders and wearing a cap with braid on the
peak.

Later when I became captain I found that
I had little time for being awesome, there
were too many damn records to keep, forms
to fill out and complaints from Seamen's
Union types to listen to.

Look at all the tiny little jobs that
those fellows who went walking around the
moon had to do. Just think - all that
expense, all that distance, just to fill
out Form-X110-347B.

Across the bay was Canada with a big

"Welcome to Canada" sign blinking across at the Americans – or was it "Welcome to Windsor", I can't remember which. I didn't want to go across the river even for an evening and the sign annoyed me, so after a couple of days of wet weather I left for Cleveland. Cleveland isn't as large as Detroit but it's just as busy, just as dirty, and just as loud as Yonge Street in Toronto – and speaking of Toronto, Ontario's pride and joy, I shall never live there again. Within the last few years, it has become a loud garish clutterbag with Yonge Street a charmless midway of cheap bars, topless slobs wobbling their moveable parts about for the slavering thrills of the Anglo-Canadian Idiot who most of the time has to get his kicks from just looking, strip clubs for the more well-heeled fools. The streets are filled with whey-faced men and cheap-looking females – one hesitates to call them women – AND they have the nerve to class themselves as "passing" Montreal and being "more daring than Montreal ever was for fun".

Balderbloodydash!!

Montreal was never tasteless. The theatre on St. Catherine that featured Lily St. Cyr had talented people – Lily included – and even the joints on St. Lawrence could give you a good show.

Toronto has become a fat, dirty old man who drools at nude tramps on tiny stages and slithers into cheap bookstores operated by rat-faced little men with rattlesnake eyes and greasy hands.

Live in Toronto – NO WAY!!

I move from lake to lake, state to state, city to city – and yet I take no joy from new places. Tourism isn't my cup of tea. Often I know I'm in a certain place because my chart tells me so. I move about because I enjoy the sailing of my boat

70

but I want to move on, never stay, never become involved. I own a small farm in Manitoba and a hill in Vermont and I am happy there but to me a city is a trap and a great bloody bore.

I dislike people in the mass and I have little use for their dirty overcrowded cities and I couldn't care less about their points of interest. During the war, I was in Paris and I never even noticed that what's-its-name tower.

Ignoring Sites and Sights is a form of inverted snobbery which I indulge in and I really believe that if most people were honest about it they'd agree with my out-look on tourism.

To sit in "Dulci's" cockpit and watch a brilliant sunset, to lie on a beach watch-ing clouds either race or move with gentle stateliness, to listen to night birds cry and to watch daybreak means more to me than looking at some great pile of histor-ical stone or a statue.

Besides, most of those places charge fees, if they were free I just might fav-our them with a visit. I hate spending money.

In Cleveland I met Duncan. He spotted my boat tied up at a rotted old wharf be-hind an abandoned tug. As a matter of fact, Duncan lived in what had once been the captain's cabin. I liked him from the start for he had the same carefree atti-tude about things as I have. For example, he liked, as I do, the soft glow and warmth of a kerosene lamp but he also liked to watch TV and you can't run a TV set on coal oil and batteries are a pain so he just ran an extension cord over to a lamppost. At the top of the post there burned a 150-watt bulb with no protecting shade. Duncan leaned a ladder - "borrow-ed from a Cleveland Works Department shed" - against the pole, climbed up, put in a double socket, and, Voilà! his TV was in business.

On the tug, he used the captain's cabin for living, the galley for cooking and the tiny mess for eating. Everything and every place he used was spotless. A former chief petty officer steward in the U.S. Coast Guard, he was fussy about things. He lived on his pension and picked up extra money doing odd jobs around the wharves for anyone he liked.

He was saving most of his pension to buy a small boat on which to travel about. He had one in mind, it was a very old Chris-Craft cruiser, a pre-war boat, it was a comfortable old tub that had had a good thirty years of reasonable care. It was up for sale but there are only a few people around who trust an old boat - try getting some outfit like Allstate to insure a boat made in 1900 with teakwood hull and rosewood decks. I suppose they look at old boats the same way one looks at an old car - with horror.

Anyway, he'd put a deposit on it and was paying it off month by month. In the meantime he just puttered around, taking life easy. Always neat and clean, he wore his old summer drills and chief's cap, a man who took pride in his thirty-five years of service; he was nevertheless pointed out to me by a man who worked in a nearby office as "one of those good-for-nothing niggers who like to be on welfare".

I might add that this character had never been in the service - he managed to grab a job in a war plant - and he was alone in his attitude towards Duncan.

I asked Duncan what he planned to do after he got the boat. His deep eyes twinkled and he answered with one word. "Live!"

All those miles had done a lot of damage to "Dulci's" paintwork and there were

still a few bugs to be ironed out. I went
to Duncan and asked his help. I knew better than to offer to pay him because we
were friends and friends do each other
favours. He came over to the boat, looked
at it a minute, then took off to where a
mobile crane sat at a construction site.
When he came back he told me to secure
everything on board because his friend the
crane operator was going to lift it out
and put it on the beach.

During the noon hour the crane lifted
"Dulci" out of the water and laid her
gently on shore. I paid the operator with
two bottles of scotch and sat back to
watch Duncan go to work. He wouldn't let
me lift a hand to my own boat.

From his store of well-used and well-
kept tools he produced an electric sander.
Within a few hours there wasn't one trace
of "Dulci's" paintwork left. For the
first time in all her long years, "Dulcibella" had a bare skin. Then he took some
sandpaper and rubbed her hull and cabin by
hand, then with a soft kiss of a touch, he
ran the electric sander over her hull once
more. Again, the hand rubbing.

He finished the final rubdown, then,
straightening up, he reached for the waiting bottle of beer. He grinned. "Now
she's ready." He looked at the sky.
"It'll be a clear night but there'll be
dew, so first thing tomorrow morning you
dry her hull real good."

He finished his beer and we went aboard
his tug to watch TV.

Early the next morning, after I'd dried
the dew from the hull, he was back at work.
Propping a ladder against "Dulci's" naked
side, he started to varnish the cabin roof.
He worked slowly, each brush stroke as
straight as a plumb line. It was halfway
through the morning before he finished the
top. He had chosen his spot for "Dulci"

73

to lie very well, we were always shaded
from the heavy sun, so the varnish would
not dry too fast.

The deck and the cockpit came next ...
he painted the floorboards off-white, the
gunnels and transom were a dark shade of
varnish.

Before he did the transom, he burned her
name and her port into her hull. Then,
while the words on the stern were still
smoking, he burned her name and number on
either side of the bow.

We went across the street for a beer and
a sandwich, talked for a while, then went
back to "Dulci".

It was late in the afternoon so we called it a day. He wanted to start early the
next day on "Dulci's" hull so that he'd at
least get one coat on before late afternoon. As we sat there talking, his crane
operator friend came over. He suggested
that, as the shed was empty and there was
plenty of room, we move "Dulci" inside in
case it rained. He even had an old four-
wheeled trailer handy. It had been sitting on its rims where the construction
job was going on and he'd thought of the
idea that afternoon.

We agreed, and it wasn't very long before "Dulci" was sitting under cover in
the shed.

Next morning, Duncan went back to work
while I prowled the war surplus stores and
Salvation Army stores of Cleveland. When
I returned that afternoon he had her port
side's first coat completed. She was
beautiful.

It took about a week and a half to turn
"Dulci" from a fat ugly duckling to a
stout princess and I was proud of her.
Duncan maintained that the boat should
stay out of the water for at least a week.
I might add that her mast now shone like
a harvest moon.

Then he dropped a bomb. He wanted to
do the inside of the cabins. I objected,
not because I wouldn't welcome it being
done, but Duncan had already spent almost
three weeks working on "Dulci" and I felt
that he had put in enough time on something for which he would get no pay. But
he wouldn't listen to me. Without the
cabin's being finished off, he felt that
it would be a half-assed job and his pride
wouldn't let him leave off.

I gave in.

It took him just three days to re-do the
interior and "Dulcibella" was ready to be
launched. Standing on the dock looking at
this beautiful boat, I felt I never wanted
to live ashore again.

I had to get moving. In a day or two it
would be August. I wanted to go to Buffalo. My new plan, instead of following my
usual inshore sailing – I'd cut across
Lake Erie to Port Stanley, then to Buffalo.
I'd make up my mind about the route to New
York when I reached the other side of the
lake.

Duncan, Alex the crane operator, me and
three glorious girls from a nearby night-
club had a party to celebrate my leaving.
The next morning, bone-tired from a sleep-
less night, I left my sepia light of lust
standing on the dock, gently waving her
bra as I sailed off to another port.

Ah me, it is ever thus with those who
follow the sea - the lakes - the rivers ...
OH BROTHER!

CHAPTER TEN

For the first time in what seemed like
months I was in Canadian waters. Port
Stanley was simmering in the early morning sun and I could hear the church bells
ringing across the water. I could see
the usual concrete government dock with
its weatherbeaten cracks and collection
of visiting yachts - mostly American. I
spotted a place and eased "Dulci" into it.
Everybody on the other boats seemed to be
still asleep so I tried to keep as quiet
as possible as I walked Belle along the
dock into town.

Port Stanley is a pleasant sort of place,
a quiet, sleepy little town with the usual run-of-the-street business section and
maybe a small industry or two. I walked
Belle a block or two, then went back to
the boat for breakfast. By the time I
returned the boat aft of me was awake.

The owners were a retired bank manager
and his wife from Toledo with a Chris-
Craft. Now, being a sailing man, I often
scorn the power boats - often referred to
as stink-pots by us "sailors" - but let's
face it, this man, at sixty-four, had only
taken to a boat at the age of sixty and to
start learning to sail at that age would
have been tough.

They had planned to retire to Florida
but after seeing hundreds of elderly people just stagnating in the sun and snarl-
ing their wait for death they made up
their minds that they'd buy a boat.

In his work as a banker he'd met the
owner of a marina, so after flying back

to Toledo they went to him for advice.
The result was a Chris-Craft named "Freedom".

I liked them. They enjoyed life and
they made the most of their forty-foot
floating home. Herb was tanned and fit
under his beat-up yacht cap and Ann was
happy in her role of "ship's wife".

They lived full-time aboard their boat,
going south in the winter and visiting
Toledo - for a week or so - while they
cruised the Great Lakes for the rest of
the year.

Watching them I was reminded of the
hundreds of elderly people I'd met all
across Canada. Many of them had found
things to interest them like boating, gar-
dening, travel, and one couple had a small
book store.

But there were many more doomed to a
remainder-of-life of boredom and sadness
because we seem to feel that it is kind
to shove our unwanted elderly into so-
called "rest homes" with such charming
names as "Twilight Rest", "Sweet Hill Home
for the Elderly", and the most sickening
of all I've ever heard - "Deserved Rest
(Homes Inc.)".

As a matter of fact, it seems to be
classed as a crime against nature if we
don't shove our retired and pensioned re-
lations into some back garden of nastiness.
One elderly lady I know runs a guest home
for fishermen and hunters. She is over
eighty-five and she gets up at five-thirty
in the morning to prepare breakfasts and
bag-lunches for them, then she cleans the
house, rests awhile and gets dinner for
as many as eight hungry men. Another
elderly lady - my neighbour - a retired
nurse, makes dolls, household items, can-
dle sticks, does church work of all kinds
and takes an active interest in just about
anything - she does all this and she is

77

slowly dying of cancer.

If you were to shove either of these
ladies in some bloody rest home they'd
die.

Herb and Ann are happy people and are
never bored and they laughed about the
friend of their son's who'd suggested that
he make them stop fooling around with a
boat and live in a proper house or the
neighbours would talk.

"Poor dears, our children are supposed
to feel guilty because their parents are
having fun." Ann sighed when she told me
this.

When I am old I don't want some evil-
meaning relation to trick me into a dismal
hole in a rest home wall. I want to be
able to sit and enjoy my old age, to sit
and puff on my pipe, read, leer at pretty
girls and watch TV. I also want to write
and paint a little, enjoy each day as a
sweet gift which is the only way to live
life.

I hung about Port Stanley for a couple
of days, then, hugging Lake Erie's pollu-
ted shore, I reached Crystal Beach. Now
there is a nice little town. It has an
amusement park for the Americans from
nearby Buffalo and other such American
centres of fun-seekers. Its Canadian
telephone and lamp poles are covered with
American signs for an American city's
civic election - Buffalo. The Buffalo
Yacht Club has its main headquarters here
- and very nice people they are too. When
I was there a fight was going on between
the Canadians and the Americans over the
right to walk on Canadian beaches that
were patrolled by American security guards.

Not being interested in the petty squab-
bles of petty Canadians - after all, they
had sold the property to the Americans and
they sure as hell welcomed American dollars in the cash registers of the taverns.

the rented houses, the park, the grocery stores, and the tax rates, etc., etc., etc. - I soon left beautiful Crystal Beach.

Now it isn't that I'm a disloyal Canadian or that I like Americans more - in point of fact, I maintain that people on either sides of the border are a large collection of large-sized pains in the ass with a few notable exceptions, but the bloody hypocrisy that Canadians exhibit when they call the Americans "hot dogs" (a Crystal Beach expression) and when our young rush about screaming at the top of their squeaky voices, "Down with American Imperialism", then rush to a coffee house to hear some Yank folk singer sing American folk songs, and when they graduate from university, take a large-paying job with a corporation with headquarters in New York, it is enough to make me want to vomit.

If we're so damned strong-minded about so-called American imperialism why don't we stop paying for cable TV so that we can watch American TV? Why don't we all buy Volkswagens instead of Fords? Why don't we eat only Canadian foods - wear Canadian styles - buy only furniture of Canadian design - collect Canadian art - go to Canadian movies - and, God damn it to hell, SUPPORT CANADIAN AUTHORS instead of loading our bookshelves with American books - AND - oh yes, let's all stop reading "Time"!

No, we won't do that - we'd rather insult some poor American tourist who came here with his family because he believed that advertisement he read in the "New Yorker" - you know the one, it says, "Welcome to Canada - The Friendly Country".

So this Canadian hoisted his sail and slowly moved towards Buffalo. I like Buffalo - I can't say why - I feel the same way about Chicago - but I like the

"It was a bit of a dirty day . . .
I could see the air over Toronto."

place. I found a spot just east of the
entrance to the Niagara River and wandered into town for the evening. I took in
a movie and a meal, flirted with the waitress in the restaurant, earmarked her for
future reference and went back to my boat.

I had to go to Toronto for a couple of
days - it turned into several weeks so I
phoned a marina at Niagara Falls and
arranged to have "Dulci" trailered to
Youngstown, New York.

I planned to sail across the lake to
Toronto. I loathe that city but I do like
money and the feel of cool, crisp Canadian
dollars in my hand helps overcome the nau-
sea that the Queen City gives me - and
Toronto is truly a "queen" city these days
for there are more queers per square foot
than in any other place except the back
streets of Los Angeles.

It was almost September and CNE time in
Toronto and that is one thing I do like
about the place - the annual Canadian National Excitation. So setting a course
bearing 300° 00' WNW, I was on my way.

It was a bit of a dirty day, not much of
a wind but it was grey and cold with a
south-east wind of around eight miles per
hour. Within a little over three hours I
could see the air over Toronto and I soon
had "Dulci" tied up to the sea-wall alongside the CNE grounds. The lakeside park
was being used as a parking lot and some
smart punk working there tried to make me
pay for tieing my boat along the wall. A
sharp slap across his unwashed face smar-
tened him up. He went whining to his
boss, an overstuffed lout with a thick
accent who jabbered about the boy thinking that boats had to pay too and "Vat vas
der matter mid you dot you should hit a
young boy, Vhy couldn't you come to see
me, der boss?"

I soon told the boss - with fine Irish

shadings - what he could do with his
bloody fat self and stalked off to the
CNE.

As usual I swung a press pass - I never
pay for anything unless I have to.   I
wandered about the grounds for a while,
went to the wonderful Marine Museum, then
back to "Dulcibella".

There was a note attached to my boat.
It read: "You are a damn englisher troub-
le-maker and if you try to cross this
parking lot again I shall get you arrest
for trespass."

His command of the English language notwithstanding, I understood his meaning
and because his sort always go howling to
the nearest copy about their so-called
bloody rights I figured I'd better find
another spot to dock "Dulci".

What did annoy me was that the insult-
ing little bastard had called me English
- may he choke on a glass of Irish whis-
key!

CHAPTER ELEVEN

It is strange that I, who hate crowds of
people, should enjoy places like the CNE
and Expo 67, but perhaps it isn't so
strange when you think about it.

A fair, a boat show, a circus - these
are not permanent. They burst into sound
and sight for a short while and then they
disappear into limbo until the next year.
People attend these affairs because they
want to get away from their lives. For a
short while they are transported from a
world where there are heartaches to a
magic place where they can be carefree.

It's an open secret that adults have
more fun at Disneyland than children do.

For a few hours even a snarl like me becomes, if not likable, at least bearable.

I had moved "Dulcibella" to where the
water show was held daily and I met an old
girlfriend who wanted to hide from her
husband so I put her up on my boat. It
was both practical and fun. I had someone to remain on the boat all day and I
had a companion at night.

Besides, I didn't like the crud she married so it was a pleasure for me to do it.
While I finished up my TV script, saw my
best friend and planned my trip, Joan lazed
about the boat and wandered around the CNE
with Belle.

As for my friend, I have known him for
over twenty years but this time I didn't
tell him about the boat or anything else.
We had a few dinners together, went for
walks, but Lionel never knew what I was

83

really doing. Why I did things this way,
I don't really know but if, when he reads
this book, he thinks back to 1966, he'll
remember that I behaved rather strangely
that late summer week - even for me.

When I met Joan on my first day back in
Toronto she took me up on the idea of living on "Dulcibella". Meanwhile, her husband looked all over hell's half-acre for
her.

One night as we watched Johnny Carson,
Joan asked me if I'd take her into the
States when I went South. She wanted to
go to Boston but she knew that he'd have
his contacts at airports, bus stations and
depots on the lookout for her. She could-
n't drive so she had to try the waterways.
I was game.

After the CNE ended I stayed in Toronto
about a week more, then off we went. We
just lazed along in the hot September sun.
We stopped at all the little Lake Ontario
shores on our sixty-four nautical miles
from Toronto to Cobourg. There are long
miles of beach and quiet and while I would
rather have had a bit of shelter when I
anchored at night, the beautiful moonlit
nights with the gentle flutter of the
water against "Dulci's" sides brought
peace of mind to a shattered young woman.

When we reached Cobourg, I checked my
handy "Texaco Inland Cruising Guide" for
a compass course across the fifty-three
miles to Rochester. I didn't want to go
from Presqu'ile Bay to Oswego because of
the Scotch Bonne Shoal that's around eight
miles out. Herb had warned me about them
and they were marked on my chart - 2061,
I think. I had a fixed keel that dug
about three and a half feet into the water
and the lake was low that year.

There may be old yachtsmen and there
may be bold yachtsmen but there sure as
hell are no old, bold yachtsmen, so the

hell with saving an extra fourteen miles
- eight miles is a very damn long way to
walk on water, even with faith.

There wasn't a hint of wind. The lake
was like glass so I filled "Dulci's" tank,
checked the running lights and off we
went. The motor would only chug along at
about six miles per hour.

The compass course was set for 143° 00'
SE. After a gentle run of a little over
eight hours with Joan spelling me at the
tiller once in a while, I spotted the tall
Rochester harbour - or as the American
charts spell it, "harbor" - light. We
anchored off the Coast Guard station at
Windsor Beach.

There is a canal of sorts running from
Rochester to the Erie Canal but there is
a large dam blocking it so that once you
are in Lake Ontario you have to go to
Oswego or have your boat hoisted out of
the water and transported to the canal.
And that's costly. Anyway it's only fifty-
nine shore-following miles to Oswego and I
like those little American towns that sit
along Lake Ontario. We stayed at Putney-
ville for four days because we liked the
food in a restaurant whose name I'm sorry
to say I forget. We stayed in Little Sodus Bay at Fair Haven for a week. By the
by, there is Sodus Bay, Little Sodus Bay,
the town of Sodus and Sodus Point.

It's twenty-four miles and six locks
going down the Oswego Canal to Three Rivers on the Erie and it took us a bit of a
while but we were the only boat going
through so we had no long, tiring waits.

Meanwhile, back at the chart I found
that there were only two locks between us
and the town of Ithaca at the foot of Cay-
uga Lake. It meant back-tracking a bit,
but I wasn't in a hurry and neither was
Joan. We checked with Belle and she was-
n't in a hurry either.

"The chart didn't show any shoals
or shallow water."

At Union Springs on the lake we almost
got hung up on a sand bank but some hard
pushing with boat hooks got us off. The
chart didn't show any shoals or shallow
water, then we learned that some idiot had
dumped several truck-loads of sand and
gravel in the almost still-running spot.

God! How can ANYBODY be that dumb?

However, the only damage was to a shirt
that got some weak American beer spilled
on it.

There is a good library in Ithaca and it
has some good stuff about canal history.

Those were stirring times when the
canals were being built and the air rang
with the singing of the bargemen.

We only stayed a couple of days there,
then we chuttered back to the Erie so that
"Dulci" could continue on her way to New
York.

The mast was battened down on top of the
cabin and there it would stay until I
reached Lock No. 1 at Troy on the Hudson
River.

There are twenty-three locks between
Three Rivers and Troy and I wanted to meander a bit - even though October was
close on.

There were a few times on the trip down
when I wished I'd been the owner of a boat
with a centreboard instead of a fixed keel
but we didn't have any real trouble and
Joan learned a few new words.

As we moved from lock to lock along the
flat countryside I pondered on the fact
that I always seemed to draw the gentle
strays to keep company with me for a while.
Daisy had been one, then I'd spent a few
days in Cleveland with a sepia-hued child
of eighteen who needed a friend who would-
n't slap her. Duncan had helped her get
a job in a hospital as a ward maid and he
planned to help her become a nurse's aide.
Now it was Joan, running away from a walking ego trip.

They shared my bed and boat, then, re-
freshed in spirit, they would depart for a
more sane, safe way of life.

I suppose that I rather like the role of
father-figure/lover but the boat always
seemed so empty after they left and because I have never enjoyed - or wanted to
be - a roll 'em and leave 'em sort of man,
I always regretted their going.

Strange to say, I am a good father-type.
In the middle of writing this book, I
paused to look after four of my friends'
children while their parents fulfilled
singing engagements.

There are some who envy me my freedom,
but freedom such as mine is often a prison harder to break out of than any place
of bricks and bars, for the prison of the
spirit can be a terrible, closed-in place
where all too often one has memory for a
companion instead of a human being.

I don't suppose that I really wanted to
see Joan leave at Albany but it was for
the best.

It didn't seem like it but we'd met
during the first week of September and
here it was almost the first of October.
A month had wandered into our lives and
passed by.

I took her to the Albany bus depot - a
real hole. I stood her a last cup of
coffee and we sat, not seeing the drunks,
the human dirt that infest the Albany
depot late at night.

The Boston bus pulled away from the plat-
form and I grabbed a cab down to the river.
Thank God the driver wasn't a talker, I
couldn't have stood it.

I was so grateful for his silence that
I broke a long-standing Conroydian Rule -
I tipped him.

CHAPTER TWELVE

I needed some shore time so I spent a few
days in Albany. It isn't a pretty town
but it does have a good library so I spent
hours sitting there reading and gently
flirting with the pretty librarians - I
like to take librarians out but you always
have to return them within three weeks.

I stayed around Albany long enough to
catch a movie that was opening, then the
next morning I started lazing my way down
the Hudson River. The autumn was really
around us, the trees were turning from
green to red and the delightful smell of
burning leaves brushed my memory with pictures of Grandfather and me raking them
up, piling them and setting fire to the
mound. The days were coolish and the
nights chilly. The old stove burned
brightly, my great double-wicked oil lamp
gave off a warm glow. I puffed away on
my pipe, read, watched TV and drank the
last of my good Canadian beer.

Let's face it, the Americans certainly
do have plenty of know-how but the beer,
except for Budweiser ("That Bud, that's
beer") - they should put it back into the
horse.

I took my time, visited towns like
Castleton-on-Hudson, Stuyvesant - nasty
shoals around that island. While I was
at Newton Hook I took a trip to Kinder-
hook to visit the House of History - OK,
OK, so I turned into a tourist for a few
days, but I wasn't part of a loud-mouthed,
camera-toting horde of yapping, whimper-
ing, complaining nits.

When I got to Kingston, "Dulci" had some of her varnish scraped off by a too curious girl in a runabout, but she was so contrite about it I forgave her. She was a school teacher with an apartment, a large man-sized chair and - unusual for a woman - decent lighting so a man could read without suffering eye strain.

I was beginning to show signs of strain and when she let me know that she was willing to let me sleep there I thought gratefully of that large bed with its soft mattress instead of my rather hard bunk.

Thoughts of comfort can oft make an adulterer out of a yachtsman faster than mere lust.

Besides, she liked Belle.

We had a charming weekend together, then I unfolded my sails and softly sailed away - into the teeth of a bloody driving rain storm. I headed for Alsen and the shelter of a small bay. Six months of sailing had toughened me up, but being cold and wet when there is shelter handy? Only a damn fool plays Hard-Nosed Salty when he doesn't have to.

The next morning was completely lacking in charm but the wind had shifted from being a dirty south wind hitting me in the face to a dirty north wind hitting me in the back. My next port of call was Poughkeepsie and Vassar College - the late Dorothy Parker, a lady who possessed a rather barbed wit, once said, "If all the girls from Vassar were laid end to end, I wouldn't be the least bit surprised."

I kept thinking of that quote every time I thought of Vassar, which was often - the thought helped keep me warm.

As luck would have it I ran into a covey of Vassar girls just as I walked Belle around Poughkeepsie's business section. Belle's bright blue eyes attracted them and within a few short minutes we were

seated in a bar enjoying a beer and I was
getting phone numbers. A weekend was nigh
and only one of the four was free, a little
redhead called Lorna.

I can tell you this, I never had a misspent youth, I was too damn busy with a
war but by golly I'm doing all I can to
make the best of a misspent middle-age.

Lorna loaded up with beer and goodies on
Friday afternoon and came down to "Dulci".
We sat talking, read, watched TV, ate
steaks and made love all weekend. When
she returned to college Monday morning we
parted friends.

She was a nice kid and I enjoyed her
company for what it was, two people who
were only casually interested in each
other but who had a need for companion-
ship. I'm not fooling myself that I
charmed her off her feet and I sure as
hell didn't seduce her. As far as Lorna
was concerned, I was something different
in her college-orientated life, a wanderer
with whom she could let herself go for a
few hours without the aftermath of the
usual crude male "Boy, did I lay that
broad" routine.

I had to get cracking. I'd met an army
sergeant in Buffalo, he was stationed at
West Point and I was to spend a few days
with him and his family at the Point.

Besides, winter was really on the way.
On Monday I said good-bye to Lorna in the
morning and hello to a snowfall during the
night. I had sixty-odd miles or more to
go - maybe closer to seventy and I was
under the weather. I didn't spring out of
my bunk in the bright mornings like I'd
done a few months before. I merely sat
up, groaned and whimpered a bit, then
crawled about my morning duties - washing,
breakfast - feeling blah.

I didn't feel like hoisting that bloody
heavy sail so I filled the tank, kicked

91

the motor into action and started off. A
few miles downriver was the small city of
Beacon. I stopped there for lunch and got
into an argument with some bird-brain that
figured I was a beatnik - they still used
that term - then he followed me to the
door of the restaurant, swearing at me and
telling me to get out of town. I was too
tired to really fight with him so I ignored his blathering and pushed my way into
the restaurant for some hot food.

As I sat reading, a cop came over to the
table and wanted to know what I was doing
in town. In a voice that crackled with
rage, I told him I'd brought my boat down
from Canada and I was sailing it to New
York. He wanted to know what happened between me and the idiot. I explained that
I'd come out of a cigar store, hadn't seen
the man, bumped into him, and before I
could say that I was sorry, he'd started
yelling at me and bothering the hell out
of me.

By this time his partner had entered the
restaurant with the man and when the first
cop asked him if I'd bumped into him, he
replied that I'd tried to attack him because I was a dirty beatnik.

Neither of the policemen would buy his
story about an attack in the middle of a
noon crowd. They apologized and took the
man away with them.

I only had a few miles to go to West
Point, or rather the town of Garrison
across the river. Bill was to meet me
there - a quick phone call from Beacon.
He had a cabin and a week's leave so we
were going to spend a couple of days just
relaxing. The cabin was near the Palisades Interstate Park. It was along the
river and it was nice to just sit in one
place, beer mug in hand, and watch the
river flow past the picture window on its
way to New York.

His wife was a pretty girl from South Bend, he was from Detroit. A career soldier, he planned on remaining in the army until he was forty - in the army three years, he was then twenty-three. He was a contented man with a nice wife, a cute child, Jamie, and a secure future.

We spent four days hiking, enjoying Betty's good cooking and some great hours of just plain snoozing in front of the fireplace.

CHAPTER THIRTEEN

As "Dulcibella" neared the end of her epic
voyage from the far reaches of northern -
well, northwestern - Ontario and the spires
of Manhattan could be seen gleaming in the
night - OK, the lights from the spires of
Manhattan could be seen gleaming in the
night - November was wafting its none-too-
gentle winds down the Hudson River from
Canada's North. My holiday with Bill and
Betty over, I pushed off. Then, with a
chill following wind, "Dulci" wended her
way along the deep cliffs that tower over
that aged harlot of a river.

At Terrytown I tarried at the yacht club
so that I could take on my last load of
supplies before New York and "Dulci's"
berth at City Island. I had about thirty
miles left of my voyage.

There is a great deal of traffic on the
river, freighters, tankers, tugs with
tows, ships of the U.S.N. on their way to
mothballs, and - once in a while - some
mad soul like me in a small yacht. I was-
n't in a hurry and yet I was. I wanted to
be done with my somewhat cramped life,
still I would be sorry when it was over.

The late Robert Maury, copy editor of
the "Cleveland Plain Dealer", had felt the
same way as his little boat "Tinker Belle"
neared England after her master's epic
voyage from the States. I'd been at it
longer than Maury - almost seven months -
and though there'd been spells ashore and
at times company, I was tired and Belle
was beginning to show signs of stiffness

94

- it was the beginning of the stroke that would kill her within five months.

Also "Dulci", old when I found her, was feeling the strain too. Her rigging was beginning to rust, the varnish was a bit blistered and the soot from the two lamps in her cabin were blackening the bulkheads. In short, the whole damn shooting match needed overhauling, refitting, repainting and the gentle hands of a warm female to stroke "Dulcibella's" master's weary brow.

I started favouring the port shore of the river as we left Terrytown. The Tappen Zee Bridge winked down at us in the early dawn, Dobbs Ferry, Hastings-on-the-Hudson, the Palisades, Yonkers. I was in a frenzy. The wind, hard aft, drove us pounding into the chop of the river. I never stopped, meals were from opened cans, their contents devoured with the aid of a filthy, unwashed soupspoon, a huge thermos of thick, sweet black tea washed the cold messes down my gullet.

By the time I reached the Inwood Hill Park and the entrance to the filthy Harlem River I think I was half-mad. I was like the lemmings on their rush to the sea, I couldn't seem to stop myself. God knows how many hours I drove "Dulci" and myself but when the lights of the Harlem River Yacht Club appeared across my bow, I gave in. I tied up at the dock, had a drink at the bar and fell back aboard "Dulci". I slept for twelve hours.

A hot shower at the club, a brisk walk with Belle, and all was well once more.

I am afraid that in my haste to get to New York I broke the cardinal rule of all good yachtsmen. I grew careless. There is no excuse for this. It was just plain stupidity. Twice on the Hudson I had placed myself in the position where I could have been run down by either a

"I could have been run down by
either a freighter or a tug."

freighter or a tug, and I remember once
reflecting rather cynically that if anything did happen, was there anybody who
would really care, but as I said before,
I was tired, overly tired. I'd been living in that tiny cabin for almost 200
days. My world was beginning to be clau-
strophobic, my temper, short at the best
of times, was beginning to break over
little things. I recall one morning bang-
ing my head on one of the cabin beams. I
grabbed up a hatchet and smashed it into
the beam. There it stuck. I dashed out
onto the deck, took a couple of gulps of
fresh air and, forgetting that the hatchet
handle was securely fixed to the beam,
walked back into the cabin, bumped into
the hatchet handle, knocked my glasses off,
and spent the next ten minutes turning the
air blue with curses.

I also recall that during that somewhat
turbulent period I actually screamed at a
pretty girl and when I do that I have to
be in a really bad mood.

That night I grabbed a taxi, wandered
around Times Square for a while, joked
with the pretty little coloured prostitutes who roam the area, snarled at a
couple of bloody queers in one of the
theatres on 42nd - these places always
seem to show action stuff like war, west-
erns and James Bond pictures.

After a show that lasted almost seven
hours - they show trailers, hold inter-
missions as well as three features - I had
breakfast, then took a taxi back to the
club. The driver was annoyed at the no-
tip I gave him ... I NEVER tip ANYBODY,
the hell with them - let 'em starve!

Let's face it, why should I support
some ill-favoured waitress and her mis-
begotten child, help pay for the beer of
some taxi-driver-cum-pimp, or better the
life-style of some bellhop.

Nobody ever tipped a writer for doing a

good job and we work a damn sight harder than these bloody grafters.

I grabbed a cup of coffee at the club-house, then down to "Dulci". Belle had a run, I checked my chart as I ate break-fast, there was about thirteen miles left before I reached City Island and my berth at Sagman's. The wind was still from the north and, added to the fun of mucking about on a filthy river, there was all sorts of river traffic like tugs in a hurry to contend with.

At least it was too cold for the brats from the slums that border the Harlem River to fire off bottles, zip-guns and other missiles if I came close inshore or passed under a bridge.

Rough weather gear on, I started the engine, put a large thermos of boaty tea in a safe place, lit a cigar, then pull-ing the hood of my dufflecoat over my head, started moving "Dulci" down towards the East River. It was snowing so I steered for the east shore, then remembered that I had to change course when I got to the mouth of the river. There was that bloody great island-park with Downing Stadium to circumnavigate.

When I reached the wide bay that is the northeast end of the East River, I really felt the force of that bloody blizzard. There was a dirty chop and the wind seemed to be shifting from the north to the east. Old Make 'n Break didn't let me down, she chugged her way along, ignoring wind, snow and my muttered curses about people who go sailing in Nobloodyvember.

Riker's Island was on the starboard side and except for some poor devils who were busy at the Pauper's Field that grim little island was lifeless. I was numb with the cold, even swallowing mugs of scalding black, sweet tea didn't help. Belle was smart, she stayed on the bunk in the warm cabin. I remembered the yacht

98

club at College Point so I steered for
there.

Six more miles to go.

The steward fixed me a hot beef sandwich
and warmed up a piece - a thick piece - of
apple pie and a damn good cup of coffee
laced with rum - HIM I tipped.

I pressed on. The wind was full in my
face now and the snow stung what little
of my face was exposed. Two bridges, then
I was out in the fury of Long Island Sound.
"Dulci" plunged and bucketed, I pushed the
throttle ahead and set a compass course
for City Island. Everything was blotted
out - this was too much - I'd head inshore. At that point in my misery I spotted the tip of City Island through the
snow, putting "Dulci" a bit to port, I
went on. At last Sagman's appeared from
behind the big Harlem Yacht Club building
and within minutes I was tied up and
shoving huge piles of bacon and eggs and
hot, hot coffee into my gut.

Except to take Belle for a run, I didn't
move for the rest of the day. Coal was
stuffed into the stove, and with the coffee pot AND the tea kettle kept hot, a
great pile of thick sandwiches and the TV
burning bright, I settled down to relax
for the evening.

I could hear the wind howling outside
but we were on the lee side of the island
so we only rocked against the dock a bit.
The fenders held firm so what was left of
the varnish stayed put.

I was tired but it was a nice tired.

Saturday was November 4th, my birthday.
I felt that it should be a joyous type of
day - I'd finished my voyage, a very large
number of miles - no accidents had marred
almost seven months, most of it single-
handed - there had been several charming
interludes with young women of varying
hues and attitudes - and it was my birthday - also I was alive.

99

It wasn't snowing, as a matter of fact the sun was shining.

Belle loved the snow but I noticed that she wasn't as spry as usual. We walked over the bridge into Pelham Bay Park. The park, on the tip-end of the Bronx, is as wild and beautiful as Stanley Park in Vancouver.

It was a cold, bright day and as it was a pleasure to be able to walk after long days of mostly sitting down, Belle plunged her nose into the snow, rolled around and acted like a cub rather than a thirteen-year-old greying wolf. After about an hour of shore-walking we returned to our boat.

The cabin was snug and the tea hot. I made my plans for the evening. There was a restaurant in the Village where the food was good and there was no idiot with a stringed noise-maker to blast at my ears - I don't like music with my meals, I usually eat with a book stuck in front of my face.

A good hot bath, my shore-going sailing-clothes laid out on the bunk and I was ready for action. Belle fed, I stalked to the bus stop and, as luck would have it, one arrived almost at once.

The long trip on the subway - this tag-end of the Bronx is the end of the line - is one of the most dismal trips in the world but at least part of it is above ground.

After a ride that took damn near an hour - give or take a grim minute or two - I arrived at my restaurant.

It was crowded and I shared the table with a rather attractive young woman. I stuck my book up in front of me, started to read, then I looked at her.

Her name was Tonka, she was a pure Apache Indian and she wrote copy for a TV production outfit ...

100

CHAPTER FOURTEEN

Tonka turned out to be a script-writer for
a company that turned out TV commercials.
She maintained that turning out the pap
every day so that millions could be brain-
washed was a good way of getting even with
the white man. When she learned that I
owned a pet wolf we became instant friends.
When we finished stuffing ourselves - this
girl ate like a lumberjack but it sure
didn't show - she produced tickets to the
opening of a play in the Village - did I
want to go with her? I did.
  The play wasn't much but it was funny
and we enjoyed ourselves and that is what
theatre-going is supposed to be about.
We wandered about the streets of the area
for a while and then I saw her home. She
lived in a loft on Lower Broadway. Now,
loft-living in New York can be one of two
ways - legal or illegal. If it is legal,
by Fire Department standards, fine - if
it isn't, you bore a tiny peephole in your
wall and when your doorbell rings you peek
through it to see if your caller is a member of the N.Y.F.D. and if your place
looks lived in the fireman doesn't get in,
but if you've been tidy and the loft looks
like an artist's studio or a writer's
workshop, in he comes, checks it out, and
if he doesn't see any signs of "sleeping
accommodation" he checks his book and goes
away.
  Of course, he knows you live there and
he knows that you know that he knows that
you live there but, there being no overt

signs of it, the man from the N.Y. fire
marshal's office is content to overlook
it.

Tonka was living in an illegal loft.

It was tastefully furnished in a rather
Spartan manner but thank God Tonka believed in chairs and there were two large ones,
one of them under what looked like a mis-
placed street lamp. Right under the large
skylight, which Tonka washed every week,
there was a big flat desk with an old-
fashioned typewriter along with all the
other working gear for a writer. The
walls - very high walls - were painted
flat white and there was a working fireplace.

The most surprising of all was Tonka's
bedroom. It was a freight elevator - a
working elevator which was used only by
Tonka (the beauty parlour on the second
floor and the store at street level had
blocked the doors off with wallboard).

Her bed was a camouflaged handcart and
her dresser was disguised as a box. A
small barrel was a chair and the mirror
was on the other side of a large poster.

Very few men have girl friends who sleep
in freight elevators.

After a glass of wine, I said goodnight,
pushed off into the New York night to find
a cab and got myself back to City Island.
The driver, a Negro, asked me if I were
an officer off a British ship, I explained what I was and we had quite a talk
about boats. When we got to Sagman's, I
invited him aboard "Dulci" and he in turn
invited me to his home for dinner on Sunday - Sunday was almost Now and I told him
that I had a date, so he cheerfully told
me to bring her along. He lived in Brooklyn and I thought to myself as I accepted
on behalf of Tonka and me that either he
had a very understanding wife or he was
really the undisputed head of the house to

be able to spring two unknown people on
her and expect her to cook dinner for them.

As I fell asleep I pondered over the
coming winter and where I'd put "Dulci".
I was of course going to live aboard her,
but while I love City Island, it is a hell
of a way from downtown Manhattan so I made
up my mind to spend part of Sunday checking out docking space near Tonka and other
areas of interest.

There was a drizzle of soon-to-be ice
pelting down when I awoke Sunday morning.
I stirred the fire to a cooking heat,
slopped down some luke-warm tea and checked my chart. Just south of the Brooklyn
Bridge is the Fulton Fish Market - that
was where I'd berth "Dulci". When I wanted to visit Tonka, all I'd have to do
would be to walk straight up Fulton to
Broadway and with a little twisting and
turning I'd be there.

It was about 0700 hours when I climbed
out of my bunk so after breakfast and
Belle's morning walk I made some thick
beef sandwiches, saran-wrapped them, filled the thermos jug with sugared tea and
made ready to cast off.

The East River is a fast river and even
in the winter there is a fair amount of
traffic so I left the sail covered, started the Beast and chuttered off for the
Fulton Fish Market.

Being me, I didn't bother to check first
about berthing but I figured it would be
alright because wharves where fishermen
hang out are always open to a man if he
knows how to behave himself.

It didn't take too long to get to the
fish docks and I was able to find a berth
that would suit "Dulci". I was in luck
because my boat was a lot smaller than the
fishing boats and I'd found a dock where
Belle would be able to get back and forth
on a gangway. It was sheltered and as

long as I remained - all winter - I never had any bother with wind, tide, people or anyone wanting to share my berth.

I never had to pay anything either.

Tonka and I had dinner with the Matthews family that afternoon and I found them a really delightful and generous couple. Mr. Matthews took us back to "Dulci's" dock, we had a drink and then we headed for Brooklyn.

Matthews lived in an apartment block that had once been married quarters for personnel of the United States Navy stationed at the Brooklyn Naval Yard. Now each apartment unit had a tile, I suppose you might call it, a reproduction of a destroyer, a battleship, a submarine, or whatever, and the families of men of these various ships - for example, all the submariners' families - lived in submariners' apartment blocks. Members of a battleship's company shared the same apartment building. A very workable plan and one which I suppose brought the ship's company closer together. However, the Navy had phased out much of the Brooklyn Navy Yard personnel. It was then in the process of being closed and the apartments had been turned over to the American equivalent of subsidized housing.

Matthews enjoyed being a taxi driver. Incidentally, he too had been in the Navy, as an admiral's steward.

The Matthews were a happy, well-adjusted couple and their children were like any children born to a family that has love in it. They had no hang-ups, there was no worrying about the drug problem except the worries that any parent has these days. The son, Jamie, was going to be an oceanographer, while Ann, who was fourteen and very beautiful, wanted to be a singer. All in all, they were a very happy family.

Which brings me to a point. If you lis-

ten to the screaming rabble-rousers, you
get the impression that every Negro in the
United States, unless he is a rich enter-
tainer like Sidney Poitier or Sammy Davis,
Jr., or a diplomat like the late Ralph
Bunche, is a put-down, sat-upon, bullied,
over-powered poor soul living in a ghetto.
It is true, of course, that there are many
Negroes living in ghettos, and put-down
and pushed around, but there are also a
great many members of the Caucasian race
who are living in ghettos and who are put-
down and pushed around. I am not mini-
mizing the plight of the Negro or other
minorities anywhere, but there are thousands upon thousands of middle-class American Negroes and Canadian Negroes who live
in complete harmony with their white neighbours and have never felt the so-called
lash of discrimination, who hold jobs,
have bank accounts, have colour TV, and
like Matthews own a perfectly lovely
little boat which they keep at a yacht
club that is about sixty-five percent
Anglo-Saxon. We have a tendency here in
Canada to make much of discrimination down
in the United States. We overlook our own
cases of discrimination, the way, for
example, the Indians are treated in Winnipeg, and I remember that the head of an
advertising agency I was doing some writing for was quite horrified that I had
brought a Negro girl to a party the agency
was holding and pointed out to me that it
was fine if I wanted to take this girl to
bed with me, but by golly, don't bring her
out in public. After all, you're a white
man and you're doing work for this agency
and you have an image to uphold.
    I might add, without prejudice, this lad
was Jewish.
    But all these screaming meamies at univ-
ersities and these organizations that make
use of phrases like "people's restaurant",

"people's library" and "people's washroom" - this is roughly translated into, if you go into a men's washroom, don't be too surprised to find a woman in there. These characters exploit the minority groups to their own noisy ends, and quite frankly I sometimes feel that they don't really give a damn about the people they're trying to help. I think actually they are more interested in furthering their own nasty ends. Of course, this is not profound or even particularly original on my part. Anybody with an ounce of common sense knows this, but unfortunately most of us have a tendency to listen to the loud noises rather than look at the quiet people of both colours who live in absolute harmony and make good livings and aren't really, really suffering.

As a matter of fact I can recall that within my lifetime newspapers in Winnipeg, Toronto, Saskatoon, no matter what part of Canada you lived in, carried ads in the classified section that suggested that if you needed a job working as a labourer, and you were Irish or Catholic, you needn't bother applying for a job there, and just after I returned from the war in which millions of Jews had been murdered, a small summer cottage resort at Bala, Ontario, had a sign sticking up which proclaimed that these cabins were to be occupied by "Gentiles only". I kicked the sign over and trampled on it. I had to pay $25 in fines and costs because of what I'd done, but I always considered it money well spent.

For the next few weeks I busied myself with writing, appearing on a couple of TV shows, resting, and on cold mornings dreaming of summer. Tonka and I spent at least four evenings a week together. I would spend a good deal of time wandering around stores like Macy's and Gimbel's -

I love the toy departments and there is a
great toy shop on Fifth Avenue, F.A.O.
Schwartz, that has trains, model soldiers
and some pretty wonderful puppets - also
some of the prettiest girls in New York
work there.

Christmas was going to be a really big
deal for Tonka and me. We were not having an affair but we did enjoy each
other's company so we planned to spend
Christmas Eve, Christmas Day and New
Years' Eve and Day together.

Then in January Tonka would leave for
Hollywood and a job with the West Coast
branch of her company. We spent several
evenings decorating the loft and a trip
to the country - the Catskills - got us a
beautiful tree. Belle frolicked in the
snow, stalked squirrels, and Tonka and I
found a delightful inn in a tiny town
called Mountain Dale.

Christmas Eve was beautiful with the
candles, the big fireplace and the lights
on the tree. Just as midnight struck we
exchanged gifts and a gentle kiss and like
a couple of kids ran giggling down the
stairs, grabbed a taxi and, of all things,
went to one of those all-night theatres at
Broadway and 42nd.

Christmas morning saw us taking a taxi
back to the loft and more opening of presents - as a matter of fact, as I write
this I am smoking the pipe she gave me.
We just lazed around the apartment, walked
Belle to the Village, had Christmas dinner
(which I helped cook), then went to Radio
City Music Hall to see the traditional
Christmas show and the usual (at Christmas) Disney movie.

The Americans don't have a Boxing Day
so it was back to work for Tonka on the
26th.

The New Year's holiday was in Boston. I
boarded Belle because I wanted to have her

107

checked over. We flew to Boston and
checked in at a little hotel that, for
the rates it charged, surprised me. There
was even colour TV in the room. It was
rather fun to sit sipping wine and watching the Johnny Carson New Year's Eve Show.
New Year's night we saw a play, had midnight supper and spent the second day of
1967 riding in a bus back to New York.

A week later Tonka was off to the West
Coast and I was on my own again.

CHAPTER FIFTEEN

With Tonka gone I was a man with more
time on my hands so I reverted to my old
way of life - work days and watch TV
every night. I had the use of Tonka's
loft because she'd paid the rent for three
years and she would be back in the fall.
The owner of the building didn't care and
I was happy to get away from "Dulcibella's"
cramped cabin for a bit.

A grateful sponsor had given Tonka a
colour TV and a hi-fi set. Tonka's collection of classical music got a real work-
out from me.

I settled into a routine of work and
fun, most of my days were spent in writing and it was a rare day that I went any
farther from the loft than the corner grocery for food or beer.

I took Belle for walks as far as the
Village, but I noted with some uneasiness
that sometimes it seemed to hurt her to
walk. I fussed with her a lot because I
had a feeling that our thirteen years together just might be coming to an end.
Every other day I would fix her a steak,
which brings me to a little incident which
I'm afraid doesn't make me look like "Mr.
Nice Guy".

One blustering January day I bought
Belle her usual steak and started home
with it. On the way I was stopped by a
bum, and I do mean bum. He had filthy
rags instead of clothes and a whine instead of a voice. He wanted money and I
never give money to anybody. I won't even

support Red Feather campaigns - I work on
the premise that whatever money I have, I
have earned, and why the hell should I
give it to anybody.

I looked at him shivering in the New
York winter and said, "Look chum, do I
look like the kind of man who would give
money to anybody, or give a damn for anyone? Bugger off, jerk, I'm in a hurry to
get home and fix this steak for my pet."

The bum looked at me and then seeing the
Canada flashes on my sailing jacket
screamed, "You Goddamn Canadian son of a
bitch, who the hell do you think you are
talking to an American like that! Why the
hell don't you go back to where you come
from, you ignorant bastard!"

Now let's face it. I'm a man who likes
to dish it out both in print and in person, but I don't like getting any of it
in return.

I grabbed him by his filthy coat and
shook him silly, then bounced him off the
wall of the building. As I walked away
from him, I could hear his filthy tongue
cursing me out.

Believe it or not, I am a compassionate
man and a kind one, but bums and drunks
arouse the worst in my nature. I inher-
ited my dislike of drunks from Grandfather
and because I have been what might be
called a bit of a loser most of my life,
the smell of these slobs - Canadian or
American slobs, I don't discriminate -
usually ends up making me rough them up.

I make no apology for this. This is me
and it's just too bad for the bums.

Would it have hurt me to give him a
dime? No. Did a dime mean that much to
me? Yes. It was my dime and I'd earned
it by the sweat of my typewriter so why
the hell should I give it to some crud who
is destined to die in a gutter.

Hard - no, I am a realist. Giving this

piece of human garbage a dime would not
have helped him, but it would have made me
have one less dime in my pocket.

So I lived my life writing and watching
TV and I loved TV in New York - it's on
twenty-four hours a day. Sometimes I'd
sit and watch movies that I had seen as a
child. At four-thirty in the morning I'd
go to bed, sleep for a couple of hours and
then get on with my work.

But I did get out of my neighbourhood
once in a while. I'd visit the Matthews
and one calm Sunday I took them for a
cruise to City Island.

I also acquired a sort of girlfriend.
It happened like this.

One Saturday I decided to go to a movie
that was playing at the Radio City Music
Hall, and let's face it, I like those vast,
tasteless stage productions that thousands
of tourists seem to spend their entire
N.Y.C. visit seeing.

Where else could you see the Easter
story represented by the precision danc-
ing of the Rockettes to the music of the
Hallelujah chorus, sung, I think, by about
7,000 people while an Easter-egg-like
thing comes out from under the stage with
a representation of the crucifixion on top
of it. By the way, I rather like the fact
that the Easter shows run from just before Easter to sometime in August, and the
Christmas show starts about November and
runs until Easter. It gives one a feeling
of solidarity that this sort of ghastly
commercialism goes on and on and on.

Anyway, back to the sort-of-girlfriend.
I put on my best jacket, my good blue
slacks, my best Wellington boots, good
turtleneck sweater, my Swedish yachting
cap, the pilot coat, and padded off to the
subway and Times Square.

Once there, I threaded my way through
the milling morons, pickpockets, relig-

ious freaks, Black Panther newspaper salesmen, cops, punks, perverts and prostitutes.

I like the triple-bill movies and the
strange little war surplus and electronic
stores where one may buy old navy gear or
a TV set new for $60 and movie cameras for
$10, when I felt a tug on my arm. It was
a pretty Negro girl - she was shivering,
and with chattering teeth she managed to
smile at me. I knew what she wanted, of
course, but she looked kind of sad and she
was lovely too, so I didn't brush her off.
After she told me the price and some of
the alleged delights in store for me, I
spoke.

"Look girl, I think you need a hot meal
more than you do a hot session with me.
Why don't we go have dinner, see a movie
and I'll still give you your fee. Okay?"

(I can hear the odd reader's reaction to
this touching little thing - "Look at this
guy, he kicks some poor hungry bum in the
mouth, but he takes a whore to dinner.")

Right - because any man who gets into
that kind of mess hasn't got the bloody
guts to get out of his own filth anyway,
but when a girl slips, no matter how much
courage she has, she is spat upon, probab-
ly by the very men who used her body, men
who figure that once a tramp, always a
tramp, so she can stay there. I might add
that women do have more courage than men
and more often than not do try to climb
out of the gutter.

It's also true that a lot of men blame
women for man's downfall.

Balderdash!

I have had a downfall or three and I
have been the one who created my own pit-
fall for me to fall down into.

A woman I will help, but a man - to
bloody hell with him.

She looked at me for a minute. There
was suspicion in her eyes - "Why do you

112

want to do that. I ain't never had nobody do that before. What's your pitch,
man?"

I explained that I just felt like it and
if she wanted to spend an evening being
treated like a human being instead of a
sex slave, I'd love to entertain her, but
if she didn't, fine.

She stood thinking for a minute, then
tucking her arm in mine, said, "Okay man,
it's your night and your dollar."

I had noticed that she was neatly dress-
ed and that she looked no different from
hundreds of pretty young office girls,
white or black, in New York.

I took her to Jack Dempsey's for dinner.
I rather enjoyed her reaction to the
place. I ordered for her because I knew
that the poor kid hadn't a clue.

After dinner was over, I asked her if
she would like to go to a play - she'd
never seen a play so she said yes. I
phoned a friend of mine who always had
tickets to any night for the sold-out
"Hello Dolly". He worked for an advertising agency. He told me to come on over,
pick them up, so away we went.

The seats were the best in the house,
third row centre.

When we came out of the theatre I could
see her eyes shining and the semi-sullen
look she'd had when I first met her was
gone. I took her to a good restaurant for
a bit of supper, then walked her back to
the cheap hotel on 44th Street where she
lived. When I tried to give her the $25
she refused it.

She asked me to come up to her room.
The white man at the desk licked his thick
lips with a dirty tongue - I think he
slobbered a bit - as he watched us go onto
the elevator.

We sat on the sagging bed talking. She
had become a prostitute because her two

older sisters were and she just figured
she would follow in the family tradition.
She had just turned eighteen, she was on
her own - no pimp - what she made she kept
for herself.

I asked her if she wanted to get out of
it. She said sure, but what would she do.

I took a good long look at her. She had
a good body - nice legs and a good face.
I had met a number of Tonka's other
friends and I figured I could help her. I
also figured she had better move out of
that hole.

I told her what I had in mind, that I
would take her home with me, let her have
the spare bedroom at Tonka's and help her
find decent work.

She was a wise child. She went along
with my plan.

She had just paid a week's rent on the
pigsty, so while she packed I went down to
get it back for her.

The fat man at the desk wasn't too fond
of giving up the rent money so I dropped
my pass card - from a Canadian newspaper
that had been closed for eight months -
and suggested that perhaps he would like
a visit from the N.Y.P.D. vice squad about
his running a bawdy house. I almost broke
his arm getting her money into my hands.
As I waited for her to come down, I took
stock of the types that wandered in and
out of the dusty lobby.

Whores with customers, sharp-faced men
with shifty eyes and a couple of big guys
who looked like tank town wrestlers.

When she came down, I gave her the money
and then we caught a cab to the loft. I
showed her her room, and we sat watching
TV for a bit, then she went to bed.

It was almost Daisy all over again, except that this kid would never have what
Daisy had - class. Sure she was pretty,
in fact, almost beautiful and she'd make

it as a model, but I hoped she'd find some
nice guy who would look after her because
she would never be more than a model for
the Village types and maybe an art school
or two.

The next day we found her a room and I
interested an art class in her. By the
end of January, Nina was making a fair
living as a model.

I just thought of something - I'm a
sailor helping the odd girl find herself,
or the odd fallen woman get up - I suppose I could be called "Salvation Navy"? ...

And I'm not in the least bit sorry that
I wrote that either.

So the days passed. Nina and I would
sit in the loft watching TV and ofttimes
making love, and I began having thoughts
of leaving New York.

CHAPTER SIXTEEN

The months slipped by from winter into
spring and I began to think about being
on the move again but I wasn't to have my
old friend with me. Belle was old and
she was sick.

One morning she tried to get up, screamed and fell over. I phoned for the vet
to come for her. Later that day he told
me that she was better off dead. I went
to see her in the cage. Her great blue
eyes flickered and her beautiful tail
thumped the floor. I buried my face in
her fur and cried. Thirteen years we'd
been together. There were memories of
walks on beaches. I remembered the young
folk singer in Toronto, her name was Tan-
nis, who had her picture taken with Belle.

I remembered thirteen years of a faithful friend and I cried for her.

I arranged to have her brought to the
boat for I wanted to bury her on Long Island in a little bay that overlooked the
Sound. A place that was ideal for a wild
animal to rest.

I left the vet's busy hospital and found
my way back to the area around 42nd Street.
I know it wasn't reasonable but I'd have
sooner seen most of the slobs in the area
around Broadway and 42nd Street dead than
Belle - I still think that way because
most of the ones who hang about the area
are queers, junkies, whores or pimps and
they are not worth one hair from the body
of a beautiful animal like Belle.

I can tell you that a large number of

people got cursed that day because of the
death of an animal. But then, most people
who live alone with an animal for a constant companion care more for the animal
than for bloody humans.

It took me almost a week to get used to
Belle's absence. I'd sailed over to the
little bay on Long Island, buried her
under a pine tree and put the headstone
that I'd carved at her head. It read:
"BELLE. A FAITHFUL FRIEND. 1954-1967."
I placed her old dish on top of the grave
and left her to sleep.

It has been almost five years and I have
never had a pet since then.

I started back to Canada and Expo '67.
I wasn't too interested in Canada's Big
Birthday or its Big Show but writing about
it for that German magazine was money in
my pocket.

Writing to me is a business just like
plumbing or TV repairing - except that
plumbers and TV repairmen get a hell of a
lot more money for their labours. It just
doesn't matter what the assignment is, if
there is enough money in it, I'll write
about it.

My last three months in New York had
been spent writing for a so-called newsletter. It was called "Warning". Its
theme - there were communists everywhere
but in Barry Goldwater's bedroom. The
publisher of this little fear-sheet was a
retired businessman who had a running fear
that somebody or some ideology was about
to take his money away from him.

In his eyes, the churches, the univer-
sities, most writers and for some unex-
plained reason all artists were RED - RED
- RED - and his readers agreed with him.

I feel that I must explain just why I
took a job with this little paper. I
don't think it was just for the money,
which was fair, but I think rather I want-

ed to get to know the type of people who believe the way the frightened readers and editors and everyone who is connected with most of the Far Right feel. In their lovely extreme way they are as revolting and as pathetic as the extreme Left.

Admittedly I was short of money. After all, one can't move around the entire Great Lakes area for seven months - even though I'd been working on articles, and making a fairly decent living - without running a little short of money. So I decided I would have to go to work. Now, there I was, a Canadian working in the United States as a writer. American immigration doesn't mind this too much unless you take a set job, and when I contacted the gentleman who ran "Warning" and told him what I had in mind, he asked me if I would like to do something on the fearful threat of communism in Canada. My first impulse, of course, was to laugh at him, but then I realized that he firmly believed Canada was filled with communists. Now there are a number of Americans, and I am sorry to say a number of Canadians, who believe this, so I decided to utilize this fearful paranoia for my own ends and write in an American newsletter about how terrible the threat of Canadian communism was to Americans.

Let's face it, the Americans have a masochistic desire to be frightened.

First of all, I knew that many Americans had believed that Lester Pearson had said, "We in Canada would rather be red than dead", when he made a speech at the United Nations regarding H-bombs and the rest of all the scare things we have these days. What had actually been said was "Many people in Canada and the United States might well rather be red than dead", but people are always taking things out of context and as my friend Lionel says, "Nobody

118

should take a man out of his context."
It may be that, after twenty-some odd
years of both being an editor and a
writer, I am still naive enough to be
somewhat surprised at how stupid people
can be. They will accept anything, almost anything that is written, they will
believe the most outrageous lies and refuse to accept the most simple truths. I
hate to feel that I am really right about
my evaluation of the human race, that the
human race is a dismal experiment that
failed several hundred years ago.

But unfortunately events have, time and
time again, proven that I may not be too
far wrong. We do seem to want to believe
the worst of just about everything and
everybody. We are too willing to believe
the cold lie rather than the warm truth.

But let's face it. I would rather be a
cynic with money than an idealist on welfare.

Perhaps a cynic is merely a man who has
had his ideals - or rather should one say
his immature idealism - crushed out of him
by the professional idealists who, to a
man, contrivingly screw everything up.

I have been a writer for a good many
years and a newspaper man for almost twenty of those years, and I have seen many
stories of human perfidy come across the
desk of a small weekly newspaper, so I
feel I have a right to be thoroughly cyn-
ical.

A letter to the Editor - I was assigned
that position - gave me a wonderfully
funny idea. The reader had the none-too-
bright idea that Canada was a communist
country so I decided to help that idea
along. Writing under the name of Thad
Dexter, I claimed to be an honest, God-
fearing Canadian who had despaired of his
country and had moved to the Land of the
Free to broadcast the TRUTH.

Working my rather strange sense of humour to its limit, I wrote that America was
in mortal danger from the North. "Canada,"
I thundered at the top of my second-hand
Italian typewriter, "has long been a hot-
bed of communist plots against the Free
World. The only people in Canada who
stand between the Free World and Red Communism was Premier W.A.C. Bennett of British Columbia, the good, God Fearing People
of Alberta and a few brave conservatives
led by Dief the Chief."

After all, didn't the Official Police of
Canada (RCMP) wear RED coats.

I worked the theme for all it was worth
and it was worth a new radio - with a marine band - a set of books, and a lot of
good cigars.

Anyone with sense doesn't believe that
sort of tripe, so I refuse to worry over
the fools who do.

Look at the record within the last ten
years. A President of the United States
murdered, and while the doctors were fight-
ing to try and save his life, a school
teacher in a southwestern state had her
pupils - it was a one-room school from
grades one to eight - applaud at the news
of the shooting. Eight young student nur-
ses were murdered by a man with a record
of weird behaviour. A young fool by the
name of Charles Black wanted more Vietnam-
ese killed. A group of young bastards
kidnapped two innocent men, murdered one,
and some of them were allowed to escape to
Cuba.

People are mugged for a bit of money -
as I was on a recent trip to New York City.
Human garbage make money selling narcotics
to children.

The whole bloody world is filled with
hate so I say, "What the hell, the whole
damned human race is an experiment that
failed several hundred years ago so why

the hell bother with it?"

Why can't I, supercynic, go find a
mountain to live on or a boat to escape
in?

Because, despite people being people,
there is still some good in the world.
There are all the sweet, young girls.
There are children playing in the sun who
just might grow up to be better people
than their parents.

There must be people who like other people no matter what their race, creed or
colour. I will admit that there are certain European races whom I despise and
look at with scorn - which only proves
that even I have human failings.

In short, for every six people in the
world who are lousy, stinking cruds,
there is one who is decent - and one out
of seven isn't too bad.

Inasmuch as this is the only world there
is I guess that I'm stuck with it so I
might as well make the best of a sad thing.
I shall continue to sail my boats until
the water is too damn thick with guck, and
live in the wilderness until some clot
with an unpronounceable name puts in a
high-rise "Let's-All-Own-A-Piece-Of-Canada"
country estate and blots out the view of
my mountain.

I shall read all my old favourite books
by men like Robert Benchley, Sinclair
Lewis, Somerset Maugham - I've read "The
Razor's Edge" over forty times - John Dos
Passos, some of John Steinbeck, most of
John Buchan, and Peter Scott's beautiful
"The Eye of the Wind", and Irwin Edman's
"Philosopher's Holiday". Of course, I
shall read, over and over again, that
classic of yachting stories, "Riddle of
the Sands" by Erskine Childers - "Dulci-
bella" was named for the boat in the book.

There are and will be other books of
course, like the book by the late Robert

121

Maury who not only sailed his twelve-foot
"Tinker Belle" across the Atlantic but
sailed it in the Muskoka Lakes in northern Ontario. Another constant companion
on all my boats is S. S. Rabl's classic,
"Boat Building in Your Own Backyard". I
have the '47 edition, there is now a later
printing of the book, this time with a
couple of new boat plans. I found it on
the shelf of my favourite Montreal book-
store.

I shall paint more pictures, smoke more
good cigars, watch TV - I am not, thank
God, an intellectual snob as well as a
standard Anglo-Saxon snob - beachcomb many
a beach, smoke my pipes, sip beer (Canadian beer) have a rum or two, and maybe
even start another newspaper - this time
I won't pick a dying town - and make love
to a beautiful, black Earth Mother who
will go to either the field or the dock,
have the baby and within twenty minutes
return to looking after me - and believe
me, I do need looking after.

That, kiddies, is real independence.

END OF BOOK - BUT WITH AN EPILOGUE:

"Dulcibella" is no more. In the spring
of '69 I discovered dryrot that couldn't
be repaired without rebuilding most of
the hull. I didn't want her to rot away
in some boatyard, to be broken up for
firewood, so I had her keel cut down to
a foot so that I'd be able to put her to
rest in shallow water.

During her long voyage of '66, I'd discovered a sheltered bay that was miles
from humankind. It was a beautiful spot
and there is a natural sea wall between
the shore and the rest of the bay. There
was just room enough to put "Dulci" into

it and the rocky shore would serve to prop
her up on either side.

Into that watery cul-de-sac I sailed
her. I spent a couple of days dragging
logs and placing rocks so that she would
rest securely. I had removed things like
the brass, double-wicked lamp, certain
books and pictures, most of the charts and
the good compass. These were left in the
hated city of Toronto.

Left aboard were certain foods in glass
jars - non-perishable things like oatmeal
and sugar. My oldest sleeping bag is
folded neatly on the bunk. There are a
few books on the shelf. The fire is laid
on in the fisherman's stove and all it
needs is a match. There is oil in the
lamps and her tattered Red Ensign (I'll be
damned if any boat of mine will wear that
bloody bikini bottom this country calls a
flag) flutters from the shrouds.

She rests, her labours of love finished.
Never again will she run free in the early
morning light. She will never again heave-
to while I check a chart.

The wind whispers gently in her rigging,
she answers with soft boaty sounds. She
dreams, and sometimes when I visit her I
sit in her cabin, I look at Daisy's picture on the bulkhead, touch Belle's old
blanket and remember all the days we had
together.

On the hot, rusting stove a great pot
bubbles - as always, "Dulci" is ready with
a pot of boaty tea.

PaperJacks

THE TRUDEAU QUESTION

$2.95 at bookstores and newsstands

W.A.WILSON, Ottawa editor of the Montreal
Star, takes a balanced but critical look at
the great political events of the Trudeau
years. The focus is on the Prime Minister
but the issues touch every Canadian.

  96 informative pages
  14 different subject areas
  large format--actual size 12" x 9"
  56 dramatic photos, many full-page size
  15 cartoons by internationally-known
    artists
  colour charts and diagrams to help you
    analyse changes in party popularity,
    the cost of living, the unemployment rate

with a COMPLETE ELECTION GUIDE including

  Riding-by-riding listing of the way the
    voting went in 1968

  A summary of the last seven general
    elections, by provinces

  The popular vote, by party, since 1953

  Constituencies won, by party, since 1953

  1968 election details on 25 key person-
    alities in Canadian politics

  54 "ridings to watch" for potential change

A BOOK FOR EVERY CANADIAN

PaperJacks

MORDECAI RICHLER

The Street

The bestselling Canadian author is at his
gamey, full-flavoured best in this lively
account of his childhood in Montreal. The
story overflows with rich humour and per-
ception that has made Richler Canada's
best-known living novelist. ($1.25)

Hunting Tigers under Glass

In this book, which won a Governor General's
Award, Richler turns his ironic eye to the
facts of life around him -- from Expo 67
through Norman Mailer, Jews in sport, Tarzan
of the Apes, and numerous other stopovers --
and finds them as strange as anything
in fiction. So he coldly and mordantly
shoots them down. ($1.25)

The Incomparable Atuk

When Atuk left his igloo for the bright
lights of Toronto and a career as Canada's
foremost Eskimo poet, he had his sights
set firmly on the Big Time . . . playing
the trend game for all it was worth . . .
setting up a profitable little sideline in
"authentic Eskimo artifacts" . . . Atuk
proved himself more than the equal of the
white men who had dispossessed his people.
Mordecai Richler, blending savage satire
and his own unique brand of ribald hilar-
ity, has written a brilliant novel of a
not-so-noble savage fallen among wolves.
(95 cents)

ONCE UPON AN ISLAND
by David Conover

Longing to get away from the pressures of
city life, the Conovers bought an island off
the coast of British Columbia, to develop
it into a small resort. This is the story
of their earnest but amateurish efforts at
plumbing, carpentry, and building, narrow
escapes from tragedy, and grim financial
struggles -- told sensitively and with humour.
A real Robinson Crusoe saga -- the adventures
of a couple that made a dream come true. ($1.50)

FLINT AND FEATHER

The complete poems of
E. Pauline Johnson

Pauline Johnson was a Mohawk Indian who
lived from 1862 to 1913. In her poetry she
expressed, as no one had done before, the
intensity and passion, the hopes and feelings
-- and much of the tragedy -- of her people.
Her poems are made to read aloud. ($1.25)

PaperJacks

ERIC NICOL

Shall We Join the Ladies?

Eric Nicol won a Leacock Medal for Humour
with this collection, which includes some of
his most hilarious pieces, such as "Sex in
the Shoe Department", "The Importance of
Being Earners", "Man's Future and Who Needs
It?" and "A Lovely Way to Die". ($1.25)

In Darkest Domestica

"Clever fun at the expense of domesticity
and all of its aspects" is one reviewer's
comment on this book which offers ten of
Eric Nicol's funniest pieces, leading off with
"When They Begin the Begats". Nicol has
won the Leacock Medal for Humour several
times. ($1.25)